THE 5 FACT FITNESS

THE 5 FACT FITNESS

Authored by
ALOK DWIBEDY

Penman Books

Office No. 303, Kumar House Building,
D Block, Central Market, Opp PVR Cinema,
Prashant Vihar, Delhi 110085, India
Website: www.penmanbooks.com
Email: publish@penmanbooks.com

First Published by Penman Books 2020
Copyright © Alok Dwibedy 2020
All Rights Reserved.

Title: The 5 Fact Fitness
ISBN: 978-93-89024-65-4

Dedication

This book is dedicated to the most important people in my life – my family. To my precious wife, Giri, you are the most abundant blessings in my life. Thank you for being my partner through it all.

To all the Teachers, who taught me the knowledge and wisdom and inspired me to be a good human being.

And yes, to the Matheran City and Sivananda Ashram, for giving me the reincarnation.

5 Facts of Fitness

1. *Exercise*
2. *Nutrition*
3. *Meditation*
4. *Relaxation*
5. *Motivation*

Acknowledgements

Before starting the fitness journey or moving to the next pages, it's my humble duty to acknowledge few people who have touched my life with their love, wisdom, expertise, blessings and energy. There are so many people who inspired me and have a significant impact in my last few years of the journey. I would love to write a few words to be grateful.

The Supreme Power, Thank you so much for your gift and helping me to realise the gift through some inciting incident! I am grateful to live a purposeful life with a mission. I am not doing anything here, through me; you are doing what you want to do.

Next in the list, I have my family, teachers, and friends. Thank you for always believing in me. You people have instilled so many values and qualities in me and always inspired me to be a good human being first.

Matheran city and Sivananda Ashram are two memorable places for me in this life. I always have a belief that I got my reincarnation in these two beautiful places. And I promise to myself to celebrate my birthday and New

Year every year in Matheran city and Sivananda Ashram. Thank you to the gurus in the ashram–Hariomanada ji, Janaki ji, Anup Sir, Prahalad ji, Nataraj ji, Saju Sir and all the beautiful yogis.

To my teacher cum friend, Vidyananda Sir and Rajan Bhai, for guiding me and giving me support in many up and down of my life. I am so thankful for the knowledge and expertise you have shared with me.

Few people inspired me and showed me the path to live an ideal life. Cricket is the religion and these two people are my god. The God of cricket, Sachin Tendulkar Sir, and our sweet Dada, Sourav Ganguly, helped me to forget my childhood difficulties and helped me to focus on my studies. The Captain Cool, M.S. Dhoni Sir, for helping me in my ups-downs of my career. The great Abdul Kalam Sir, for showing me the power of patriotism and dedicate the life for the service of others.

Khiladi star Akshya kumar and the handsome John Abraham for teaching me the discipline and perseverance and inspiring me to be fit and healthy. Thank you to the two beautiful ladies for the inspiration–Manisha Koirala mam and Susmita sen mam. Love the way you people are living your life. Truly inspiring!!

Thank you to the leaders and friends–Tom Bilyeu, Gary Vee, Lewis Howes, Kobe Bryant and Peter Dinklage. It's because of you, I could quit my job and working on my passion. See you soon in the shows guys!!

Thank you to all the inspiring leaders and authors for your beautiful words–Tony Robbins, Jack Canfield, Bob Proctor, John Maxwell, Brian Tracy, Les Brown, and Robin Sharma.

Thank you to my publishing and editing gurus–Kailash Pinjani and Deepak Parbat. You people did a great job by converting my research and thoughts to this beautiful piece.

Finally, to you, the reader: Thank you for believing in me and my work. No idea works unless you do. Now it's time to promise me you will apply these 5 facts in your life to be healthy and fit. Yes, don't forget to share these ideas with others so that, we can make ourself healthy, our family healthy and our society and country healthy. Let's connect in social media pages and keep sharing the greatness!!

A Note to YOU

No matter whether you are in your 20s, 30s or 40s, it's time to work on your health. And you are reading this book is the proof that you want to change your current health status. You need to save a lot of energy in your personal account to enjoy the later part of your life. I congratulate you for choosing the different path and would like to become your personal coach for the upcoming health and fitness journey.

As a health and lifestyle coach, my job is to give you simple and executable health and fitness tips and techniques to improve your health and energy. My goal is to make yourself healthy, your family healthy and your society and country healthy. The number one thing I would like to share with you is, please understand the difference between information and knowledge. Information is cheap and easily available nowadays for the vast social media. You need to apply the information in your life and convert it into knowledge with your experience and learning. Once you have the knowledge, please don't keep with you. Start sharing with your friends, family, and near ones.

Remember, "Health is a choice. Energy is the new currency". And this book will help you choose healthy and enhance your energy. It's not a casual promise, the concepts of the book are already proven with my personal clients and in my both the start-ups. This book will give you immense benefits even if you are super busy in your life. Go to every chapter end to revise the basics of the chapter and complete the 5 week fitness plan. While following the fitness plan, if you face any queries, you have two options to do. One is to go back and read the chapters of the book or contact me or my team in any of the social media platform given in the let's connect page.

One last thing before starting our health and fitness journey is, please remember in every area of your life including health and fitness, consistency is the key. Don't lose the path. If lose, try to come back again and again. Many of my clients lose several pounds many times with me. Thank you for choosing me your coach and being part of my mission. Let's start for the updated version of you together!

With health and love,

Alok Dwibedy (AD)

My Story:
The Inciting Incident

I opened my eyes slowly and saw three people were sitting beside me and discussing something. One was my newlywed wife and two of my friends from my hometown. I wasn't able to hear what they were talking. The same old lady who gave me a blessing yesterday was crying and praying God in the opposite bed. I tried to wake up and turn around in the bed and felt a terrible pain in my left hand and armpit. "Ahhh", I shouted. My wife came to me and asked, "What happened, are you okay?" I replied with a painful Yes and smiled to see my friends.

"What's the time Mam?" I asked (yes, I called her Mam)

"It's 6.30 evening." She told.

A nurse, Sujata, came and announced that doctor is coming for evening check-up and make sure only one person is allowed with the patient. All other people please vacant the room. Mam arranged a pillow so that I can sit and keep my left hand over it. Doctor came with one of his assistants and two nurses and started checking the patient beside me. It took him 5-10 minutes then it was my turn.

"How are you feeling now?" Dr. Veer asked.

"I am feeling little weakness and terrible pain in my left side of the body," I replied.

"See, Operation was successful and may be because of that stitching, you are feeling the pain. Nothing to worry," he replied and asked for the file to the nurse.

"Hey Alok, your biopsy test report will come in next 2-3 days from Mumbai, and we are guessing it's just a lymph node infection. Keep taking food and medicine on time." He told and moved towards the Bed No.3 after giving the file to my wife.

I saw my innocent wife and her worried face. She was busy in cutting an apple for me. My friends came and told bye to both of us from the entry gate and left. Mam gave me the apple and a banana and asked me to take the prescribed medicine. Then she helped me to go to the bathroom and change my dress. We spoke to family members over phone and told them "everything is fine here", which wasn't true. We both were thinking in our mind about the biopsy test report with tremendous fear without showing each other.

Around 9.30, I had my dinner, and she was ready to leave as there was no facility for staying in the hospital with patients. She discussed with the nurse for another 5 minutes and came back to me exactly the same way like other 9 days. Yes, it's my 9th day in the hospital bed. She showed me the extra blanket and gave me my journal and book and then left. I started reading the book "The immortals of Meluha" but unable to focus as many thoughts came to my mind.

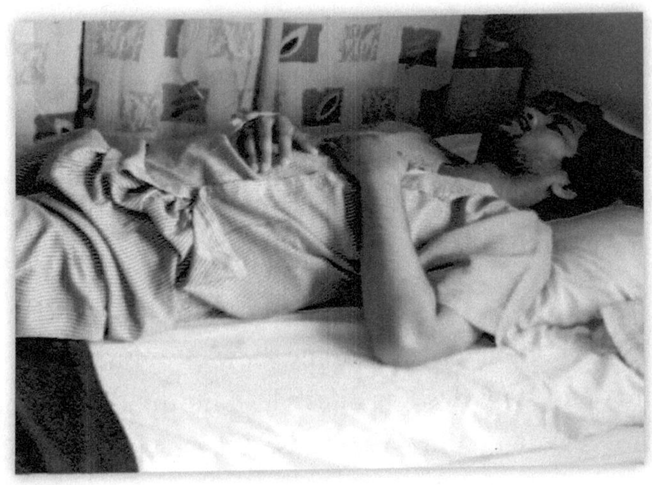

It was 15th May, 2015 and Friday. While my friends and colleagues were busy in their weekend party, I was lying on the hospital bed with terrible pain and waiting for my Cancer test report. I was thinking about my wife and family that what would happen to them if I have cancer and died after some days. Oh gosh, I am getting goosebumps now thinking about that day. On that day, the only thing I required in this world was my health, not loads of money, or a beautiful bungalow or any exotic vacation. I went to bathroom again and thought who's responsible for this kind of situation and recalled my last three years of unhealthy corporate lifestyle.

A little Back-Story

I am from Bhubaneswar, the capital of Odisha, a state still unknown in metro cities. People here in Pune and Mumbai ask me sometimes, "Odisha! Where is it?" And I reply, "It's in Mars and just discovered by Elon Musk". In my hometown, I had a very active lifestyle. I played Cricket at least 5 days a week and went for a long relaxing walk with my school and college friends. In 2012, I came to Pune for my job search and in the next 6 month I got a job in an MNC as an Application developer. This was the start of my sedentary and not-for-living-but-for-dying lifestyle.

It was completely new to me–new city, a new job, new friends and new desktop lifestyle. Life divided into two parts–Weekdays and Weekends. I spent around 10-12 hours daily in front of my laptop whether in my office or at home. And the most critical part was corporate and weekend parties. I called them "Party for no reason". In those three years, I rarely played my childhood favourite game and went for any long walk. So, sedentary lifestyle, junk food, unhealthy practices results into that terrible medical condition.

It was already 11.30, and I could not sleep. Suddenly I saw the picture of God and Mother Teresa on the wall and cried like a baby. In that very moment, I promised to the God, The Almighty, Supreme power, if you would give me a second chance to live then I will never compromise in my life in these three things, "Health, Relationship and

Career". I will truly live instead of just breathing. We often ignore our health for our so called busy life but on that day I understood the real meaning of, "Health is true Wealth".

Post Hospital Tragedy & Depression

On 18th May, The report came, and it was good. It was just a lymph node infection and swelling. After a series of check-ups and formalities, they discharged me. On the very next day, I went to my hometown and stayed there for a month with routine check-up in a local health clinic. Family and relatives came to see me and it was a kind of family get together. But in my mind, I thought about that promise I made to God on that day and grateful for giving me the second chance.

Life was difficult for me after the recovery. Whenever I saw my bare body, and that operated mark on my armpit, I thought about that terrible period of my life and stressed a lot. One day, I woke up in the mid night and went to the balcony and started breathing deeply. I thought I was dying, and it happened many times. I went to a doctor, he gave me some medicines and everything was okay after that.

In the year end time, my sister-in-law came for a vacation. She is a doctor. She asked sarcastically, "Bhai, What happened, are you in depression?"

"No, why did you guess so?" I replied. And I had no idea that she already checked my medicine.

"See, this is an anti-depressant." She told.

She showed me in Google and I was surprised to know that I was in depression. I knew it all happened because of that medical incident. With no delay, I applied for a quick leave and went to a nearest Hill station Matheran–Asia's only automobile-free hill station. And those 4 days was life changing for me. You can say my reincarnation or second-birth type.

The Life Changing Moment

I spent my small vacation in complete tranquillity and enjoyed the beauty of nature with my wife. I avoid my cell phone in those 4 days and read a beautiful book "The way to peaceful warrior". After coming back from Matheran, I joined a Gym close to my home and started working on my physical fitness. It's a well-equipped Gym with many facilities like Yoga, Bollyfit, Zumba, and Swimming.

The next issue I faced in my fitness journey was diet and nutrition. My trainers & friends confused me with their so-called *'free-advices'* like, "Eat 16 eggs a day to get the protein"–My wife became mad one day to see me eating 8 eggs in my breakfast. "Buy this/that Whey Protein and Mass Gainer,"–I bought that too. To clear my doubts on this, I started learning Diet and Nutrition from different books and lessons available on Internet. Later I joined a course and become "Fitness Nutrition Coach". By working with some clients in the beginning I got to know that dieting is temporary and what important for us to focus on Lifestyle changes. Hence, I researched a lot on this subject and became a "Health & Lifestyle Coach".

One day, I was feeling little weak in the gym because of the overnight stressful project delivery in my office and my trainer realised that...

"Alok, what happened!!? You are not in the flow today," he asked.

"I am feeling tired and not able to give my 100%" I replied and left the lat-pull machine.

"No worry, take rest or you can attend the Yoga class which is about to start. It will be good for relaxation and stretching,"–He told me and left wishing me Good luck.

I waited there for 10 minutes then attended a 45 minute Yoga class on that day. It didn't take me enough time to realise the magic of Yoga in our life. While lying on the yoga mat, I read the quote written inside the studio saying "Do Yoga–It just makes Life Better". Because of the morning yoga session, I felt relaxed and energetic throughout the day. Later, I started learning more about yoga and its benefits. I anxiously waited for the next class and then after the class met the trainer Miss. Rupa. She's superb and had a clear understanding on her subject. We discussed close to 30 minutes there on different topics like Yoga, its benefits on body and mind, how she found Yoga, Yoga classes and retreats in India.

After that I changed my normal vacations into Yoga and Meditation Retreat which includes Yoga, Meditation,

Nutrition, Ayurveda, Fasting and Detoxification. In the last 4 years, I visited several Ashrams and retreats in India and met many peoples to know more about health and wellness. I become a Yoga trainer and Juice Therapist. I researched and read more and more about ancient philosophy and modern medicine.

It took me 4 complete years to find the perfect recipe of health and fitness. I started sharing the things with my friends, family and colleagues and felt super happy to see the results. Few months back, I quit my corporate job and started working as a Health and Lifestyle coach. On request of a friend cum client, I am writing this book to share my research and knowledge on health and fitness, **The 5 Fact Fitness**.

Let's start the Fitness journey together...

Introduction

What is Five Fact Fitness?

Facts

In 2017, while working on my research paper, "Lifestyle and diseases," I found a new name for our country, "Diabetes Capital of the World". India and the USA are the top two countries in the list. Over 70 million people are suffering in this lifestyle disease. Not only diabetes, but a similar situation with all other lifestyle diseases like, Cancer, Cardiovascular diseases, and Depression. In depression and suicide, again our country is at the top of the list. As second largest populated country with 1.3 billion people, while we are struggling to get a single gold medal in Olympics and officially ranked 67th at Rio Olympics, We are in the top positions in these diseases list.

I completely agree that some external factors are affecting our health: pollution, pesticides/chemicals used in our food, lack of proper healthcare services, and contaminated food/water. However, one thing we all know that we have a wonderful smartest machine of the world which works 24*7 named as "Human Body" and protecting us from all these toxins. If not so, then imagine what would happen to us after smoking just one cigarette. It's our body that protects us from all these mischiefs by its magical operations. And it just expects only one thing from us. From our end, we must take care of it and by doing this; we can easily avoid about 90% of all these health issues.

Why 90%? Because– "Health is not Physics"

Yes, I mentioned it right; it's 90% not 100. Whatever you try to do to take care of your body and mind, you can't guarantee the absolute health condition as it's not proven as physics. If you throw a ball to the sky, then it will definitely fall down after a while because of the gravitational law of physics and it's proved. But still you need to take care of our body to maintain regular health and energy. And 90% is not a bad score.

The Funniest thing is - We know everything

From my quick health awareness survey in 2017, I got a funniest thing - we know everything and well aware of it but we are not doing anything. And we have a series of excuses for that. Remember, you have to take responsibility of your health.

"You can't cross the sea merely by standing and staring at the water."

—Rabindranath Tagore

Choice and Little thing matter

Every moment of every hour of every day, you face different choices. What to eat what not to eat, what to do what not to do, where to go where not to go. You can take a simple positive action or negative action depending upon your decision on those choices. These simple actions, repeated over time, will determine the life you lead. Little things matter. Little things that lead to success are easy to do. Small actions compound over time. For example, if you exercise for an hour a day, you won't see much difference after a couple of days or even a week. However after a few months you will notice a big difference. A little effort each day will result in huge rewards.

In my last year retreat I met a wonderful human being and had time to discuss about his life. He was a doctor in Mumbai 2 years back. Because of his hectic medical schedule, he could not give some time to himself. On top of that, he was running a private clinic. He told me on that day, " I knew everything. I had to take care of my body and mind but unable to spend even 10 -15 minutes a day in solitude. I became overweight and terribly stressed. One day, while coming to my hospital, I faced my first heart attack in the parking. After that believe me I became responsible for all my choices. I left the hectic job and only worked from my private clinic with total peace and harmony. Now, I am taking care of my body and mind. And am also, teaching the same in my clinic to all my patients to do so. I have added Yoga and meditation in my clinic for all my patients and relatives for Free. Believe me Alok; we know everything but still waiting for the awakening moment in our life." After knowing his life-changing story, I just replied to him, "nice to know your story. It inspired me to work more on my health and fitness research. Similar kind of incident happened with me also."

Knowing is not the same as Doing [Information vs. Knowledge]

"If information is enough, then everyone in this world would have a million dollar bank account with a six-pack abs."

—*Anonymous*

Knowing how to do something and doing it are two different things. In this digital world, Information is cheap, easily available but knowledge is rare. There is a huge difference between Information and Knowledge. If you try to find in the internet and libraries, you will find thousands books on how to become rich and how to have a six-pack abs. However to get a million dollar or a six-pack abs, you have to do the hard work with right kind of mindset and discipline. From the book you will get the information and experience of great people but you have to make the strategy to apply that information and convert them into knowledge with your experiences.

You are reading this book now means you want to improve your health. Yes, only you can improve your health, nobody can do it for you. Your body is the only place to be live in this beautiful world and the only vehicle to travel the journey called life. So, before buying your dream bungalow and car, first take care of this one, your only home and vehicle. As we know, we can buy/replace the bungalow and car many times but for this body, no buy/replace option. Before reading the book further, I request you to tell this line with me– *"I will take care of my health from today onwards."* Even to make it more profound, find someone now in your family/office and say the above sentence to him. This is the only way we can make us healthy, our family healthy and our society/country healthy.

"You can't hire someone to do push-up for you."

—*Jim Rohn*

Personal Health Account

Our health is like a bank account, I named it as Personal Health Account. By working on it daily with some exercise, mediation, sleep, proper diet, you are making regular deposits into it. But when you sit too much, eat too much junk, and living an unhealthy lifestyle, you make withdrawals in your Health account. See, there is no plateau state while talking about your health, either you are building it or decaying it with your every choices and decisions. In yogic principle, they call it, "3 Phase period". Our life goes through 3 phases and 4 points.

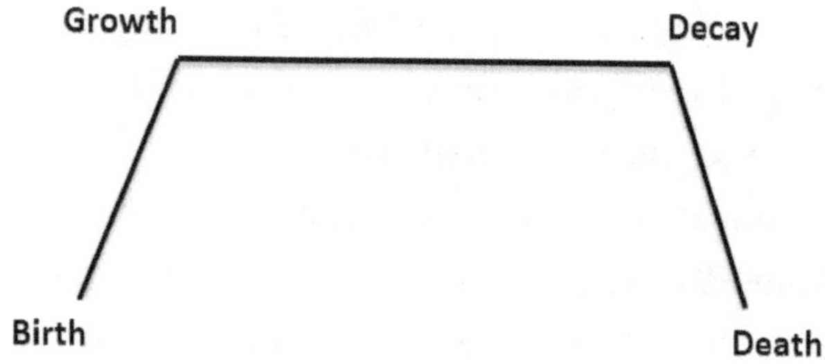

The Growth phase starts with Birth Point and end with Growth point. In this phase, our body and all our organs are in a growth mode. The plateau phase starts from Growth point to Decay point. In this phase neither body is in growth mode nor decay mode. The Decay phase starts from Decay point to Death point. In this phase the body starts its decline. The plateau state seems like idle but it's actually either in building or decaying mode. By taking care of your health in this period, you can enjoy life in the decaying period. Like our Yogis, instead of spending life in pain and suffering with diseases, you must enjoy the decaying period with a healthy body and mind.

Five Fact Fitness

For Health, the very first thing comes to our mind is to join a Gym or diet. And we define health is just the absence of disease. WHO defines health as, "Health is a state of complete physical, mental and social wellbeing not just the absence of diseases or injuries." To be Healthy and Fit, we need to take care of all areas of health and fitness: Physical, Mental, Emotional, Spiritual and Environmental. And to do that what you need is a robust system with all the basic elements–Five Fact Fitness.

A. Exercise

Exercise is a miracle drug. That's why it is in top of the list. By exercising daily and moving more, we can prevent many lives-threatening diseases. Exercise has many more benefits apart from weight management like improve memory and concentration, relieve stress and anxiety. It is one of the best anti-depressants and anti-aging elements.

B. Nutrition

We always heard, "80% diet, 20% exercise", "Food is the best medicine", and "Abs are made in kitchen". Yes, it's true. After movement, the next most important fact in health and fitness is Nutrition. It's important to focus what you are putting in your mouth. Understand and aware about all the macro and micro nutrients. Ditch all the junk and drug foods available in the market. Cook your own food. Feed your vehicle with the best possible fuel, not the cheaper one.

C. Meditation

Exercise is for body and Meditation is for Mind. Our mind is a terrible master but a wonderful servant and it works like a Monkey [we call it Monkey-mind]. Your mind processes about 60,000 thoughts every single day and these thoughts and beliefs majorly affect our health and energy. First you need to understand where your thoughts come from, how they arise. Healthy body and peaceful mind are two basic sources of energy and by practicing meditation daily; you will have a peaceful mind with awareness and willpower.

D. Relaxation

When the body and mind are constantly overworked, their natural efficiency diminishes. In our so called busy life, it is very difficult to relax and spend some me-time. Many have been forgotten that rest and relaxation are nature's way of recharging. Now, we are making our vacations and off days more hectic and stressful than our regular work days. Practice Yoga and Deep breathing and avoid at least one day in a week all the screens. Every day set a time for physical, mental and complete relaxation.

E. Motivation

In some phases of your life, sometimes you feel down. You need someone or something at that moment to uplift and get the momentum again. You face many setbacks and failure in your day-to-day life and to come out of that what you need is Power of Motivation.

Know your why–Ikigai, the reason for being. By having a career fulfilment, you can avoid all the stress and tension from your job life. Spend time with uplifting people and read motivational contents every single day.

How to Use This Book

I know that Health and Fitness books and contents are easily available and coming in thousands. I never wrote this book as a Health and Fitness Book. After the four years of research and helping many people, I wrote this piece that you hold as the complete formula for health and fitness. Please don't misunderstand me. I don't claim to be an expert on these subjects. I consider myself a "Work-in-progress" and I continue to learn every day.

The first two chapters in this book is just an intro of me, my story and my book for you. The next five chapters will give you a thorough understanding of the concept–Five Fact Fitness. Don't skip any chapters, read it in sequence. Once done with all the chapters, follow the fitness challenge and lifestyle program in Chapter-6 and 7.

The most effective way to read this book is,

- Read every chapter in sequence

- Do the exercise /task after every chapter

- Discuss with friends, family and colleagues after every reading.

- Follow the 5 week fitness challenge and the lifestyle program.

In case any doubts or confusion while reading or discussing with others, please free to contact me in the email or comment your question in social media platforms. You will start a life-changing journey that will bring health, energy, success and happiness.

Let's get started...

Contents

EXERCISE

"Sitting is the new smoking.
Exercise is a miracle drug, take it every day."

—Alok Dwibedy.

"Exercise is like telling your body, "you're gonna hate me
for this, but you'll thank me later"."

—Anonymous

What your favourite stars do first thing in the morning? What is constant in their morning ritual? Yes, it's Exercise. From your favourite celebrities to world-class sportsman, from great CEOs to famous speakers, all prioritizes health on top of their list. They all start their day with a strong exercise routine. They already realised that money can't buy health. Yes, the bank balance, relatives, and insurance companies can pay the medical bills, but what about the pain, time and the most important thing – their mission? Dwayne 'The Rock' Johnson starts his day before 5 and hit the gym first thing in the morning. Pinkathon (a special marathon for the women in India) ambassador, the Ironman Milind Soman always adds barefoot running, trekking and Yoga in his morning ritual. Tony Robbins, the No.1 self-help Guru starts with a special workout plan with his personal trainer followed by a cold-water bath. The greatest Olympian Michael Phelps, Tennis star Roger Federer, Apple CEO Tim Cook, media sensation Oprah Winfrey, they all start their day with Exercise. Exercise is a best way to start the day with high energy and full of enthusiasm for these top world-class performers. Let's learn some wonderful tools and techniques to add this miracle drug to our lifestyle and convince our mind to do it every day.

Let's move...

Exercise is a miracle drug

Exercise means to move our body so that muscle works and burn calories like Strength training, Cardio, Yoga, Pilates, and Tabata. Movement is life. If you are not moving,then you are dying. Your sedentary lifestyle makes you lethargic and killing you silently.Now, we are living a box lifestyle. Waking up in our home checking our phone first thing, then going to office in our car then spending a wholeday in the cubicle in front of our laptop and coming back to home, watch TV/Netflix and then again back to the room. There is zero movement in our life. And the funny part is we are watching 'how-to-lose-weight' or 'how-to-be-fit' videos in YouTube while sitting at our desk and eating pizza and soft drinks.

When we were hunter gatherer, then what was our day-to-day lifestyle? Just imagine, throughout the day moving from here to there to gather our food and then prepare the food and eat with the whole community. But now, we are getting food in a click. The online platforms make the situation more dangerous as we need not to go out of our room to have the food. There is a misunderstanding in most of the people (I found with many of my clients) that we need exercise when we have to lose some weight on a doctor's recommendation or to wear that beautiful marriage dress in the party. I have some clients who lose some weights several times. See, exercise is a miracle drug as it has many benefits apart from weight management. Take it every single day in any form.

Boost the memory and improve concentration

Your brain remembers more when your body is active. By increasing the supply of oxygen into your brain, exercise helps to boost the memory and reduces memory loss. Hippocampus, the centre of the brain's learning and memory system, responds well if you do regular exercise especially aerobic exercises like walking or cycling. When you exercise, new brain cells are born in the hippocampus. Also, by regular exercise you can increase your attention span by avoiding the distractions.

Stress reliever & mood enhancer

Exercise helps to improve your mood and decrease feelings of depression, anxiety and stress. It creates some happy hormones like, serotonin and endorphins. Serotonin relieves the feelings of anxiety and depression. Endorphins help produce positive feelings. Regular exercise help you relax and sleep better. In addition, after exercising even for a short-period, you may feel a sense of accomplishment and your muscles will feel more relaxed.

Fitness and weight management

Exercise plays a big role in our daily total energy expenditure (TEE). A one hour of light to moderate workout burns 200 to 300 calories and helps us to maintain our ideal weight. There are two types of weight, Muscle mass (good weight) and Extra Fat (Bad weight).

The professional bodybuilders are super healthy because of their muscle mass irrespective of their size and weight. Exercise like strength training helps us to improve our muscle mass and removes the body fat. To be fit, you must have an ideal BMI (Body Mass Index) and Body fat percentage. Through regular workout, you can maintain your ideal weight, BMI and Body Fat percentage. Also, Exercise helps to increase your energy level.

Anti-aging

Once you crossed the age 30, your muscle loss occurs faster. Age-related muscle loss, called sarcopenia, is a natural part of aging. After age 30, you lose as much as 3% to 5% per decade. Less muscle means greater weakness and less mobility, which increases your risk of falls and fractures. Regular exercise helps to reduce muscle loss and thus strengthens the muscles. Just as exercise strengthens muscles, it also strengthens bones. Exercise can reduce the rate of bone loss and build bone density. So, you can prevent Osteoporosis.

Prevention of life-threatening diseases

By doing regular exercise, you are protecting yourself against many lifestyle related chronic diseases. It improves your overall health and fitness level. Regular physical activity protects your heart and lungs functions, improves flexibility of muscles and joints, and increases energy. It decreases blood cholesterol, blood pressure, cardiovascular diseases, cancer, depression, stress and anxiety.

Common Excuses of not doing Exercise

"There are only two options:
Make progress or make excuses."

According to latest research from an agency, they found that almost 64% of Indians don't exercise. They are very much aware about the importance of exercise and want to live a healthy lifestyle, but lack of motivation and time make it difficult for them to do regularly. In 2018, I did a research by asking few questions to my friends, family and colleagues about exercise. I found that over 70% of them don't do any kind of exercise and the main reason for that is 'do not have enough time'. And the same people spend a 2-3 hours on social media and TV every single day. Lack of time for not doing exercise is not a valid reason; it is just an excuse. Apart from this, I found some other excuses, but this one is the major.

I don't have time

The health coaches and fitness experts say you only need to get 30 minutes of exercises per day and five days a week. And that is, 30*5 = 150 minutes per week. It's not too difficult to get 2.5 hours out of 168 hours for living a healthy lifestyle. We rarely focus on these small little things in our life. Later, these small things are changed into a do-or-die situation. Remember, "Little Things Matter". Also, we can separate those 30 minutes into two 15 minute morning and evening session.

I don't have equipment/facilities

You don't need to buy any equipment and join costly gym or health club for doing exercise. What all you need is Willpower. As I always say to my clients, "Exercise is a miracle drug and your body is the best gym. Take this drug every day in any form". You can do body weight exercises, Yoga, walking, running, cycling, stair climbing, gardening and many more exercises. Nowadays, many online videos are available from different fitness coaches for free. You just need to watch the video and follow the instructions carefully.

I am not a morning person

See, you don't need to wake up 4.30 in the morning to go for a walk or do any exercises. That's for professionals. To be fit, who said that you have to do exercise only in the early morning? Do at least 10-20 minutes of quick exercise as soon as you wake up. It will improve the blood circulation and secrets some happy hormones to give you a best start of your day. Also, you can do some kind of exercise after your daily job. It will release all the stress and anxiety and help you burn some additional calories.

My weight is fine

Some people only exercise just before their marriage or any defence job selection. Friend of mine joined Gym and lost 6 kgs before marriage to just wear her beautiful marriage dress, and again gained 8 kgs in just 6 months after marriage. Exercise is not only for weight loss. It has many more benefits: improve memory and concentration, enhances mood by releasing some happy hormones, anti-ageing, and protects us from many life-threatening diseases. So, irrespective of your weights just do some kind of exercise every single day.

I am too old to start

In my yoga and meditation retreat, I saw many old people and they are super fit and healthy and ready to do even advance asana. There is no such age limit to start any fitness program; it's all there in our mind. You just need to be aware about your current health and start a fitness program to get the health and flexibility back in few months. My mother-in-law is suffering from many health conditions from last 6 years and she is just 64 now. While suggesting her to follow any exercise program, her reply is same from last 6 years, "I am too old to start".

> *"If you want it, you'll find a way.*
> *If you don't, you'll find an excuse."*

Types of Exercises

This is a very common question I faced many times in my coaching classes and seminars, "Which exercise to do–Is it running or cycling or yoga or weight training? I don't know how to start". As part of my research, I met many fitness trainers and health coaches and we discussed on this topic in details. Our discussion covered very ancient exercises like Yoga, Tai-chi, and some traditional martial arts to the latest exercises like Tabata, Zumba, and HIIT. What I found is, Types of exercises may vary but the fundamentals and basics are always being the same. You need to understand the basics and fundamentals first before choosing your exercise plan.

There are 5 types of exercises you should include in your fitness program. You should always start your exercise program with a basic warm up routine and end the program with some kind of cool-down exercises. And whichever exercises you know can come under these 5 basic types.

Warm-up Exercises

Warm muscles work better than cooler muscles. Warm muscles deliver more oxygen to muscle fibres and it increases elasticity of the muscle tissue. Proper warming up the body increases the muscle temperature and the flow of blood in the muscle, all of which decrease the *viscosity* (internal friction within the muscles). Hence, you must do some warm-up exercises before doing your regular exercises. For weight training, you can do some push ups, pull ups, toe-touch, jumping jacks to give the warmth to the muscles. In case of Cardio exercises, you can start slowly before moving to high intensity. For Yoga or any other flexibility exercises, you can do Surya-Namaskar and some basic leg stretches. Do the neck stretching and joint rotation before moving to any exercises to avoid the injuries.

Strength Training Exercises

One of my clients said to me, "I am doing yoga. I don't like to go to gym and do weight training". It's not about like or dislike, it's about what right to do. Once you become 30, your muscle loss happens faster. To protect that muscle loss, the best way is strength training and taking care of your protein in your diet. If you have the facility of Gym or Health club,then do some weight training exercises. Else, you can do various body weight exercises at home like push-ups, squats, burpee, plank, and wall-sit. Also, you can buy a pair of dumbbell and kettle bells to enhance your training experiences. Kettle bell workouts are powerful; learn the techniques from the professional or experts.You should do at least 3 sessions of strength training per week covering all the muscle groups.

Cardio Exercises

Cardio stands for cardiovascular exercises. As the name suggests, it is best for your heart health. It increases your heart and breathe rate. It has many benefits to our body: maintain a healthy weight, increases stamina, boost immune system, and strengthens your heart. The best form of cardio exercises are walking and running. You can do in your gym or home with your treadmill or you can do outside in open air. The other form of cardio exercises are cycling, swimming, stair climbing, elliptical, and jumping rope. You should do a minimum 30 minutes of cardio exercise 5 days a week to make your heart and lungs healthy.

Flexibility Exercises

Flexibility exercises stretch your muscles and can help your body stay flexible. These exercises may not improve your strength or endurance, but being flexible gives you more freedom of movement for your day-to-day activities. Here by saying flexibility exercises, I mean mobility, flexibility and balance exercises. The best form of this type of exercises is Yoga. Yoga has many basic to advance asana which challenges your current flexibility level. Find a Yoga trainer and start practicing the asana to become more flexible. Do some basic asana, mobility steps and balance exercises 3 to 4 days a week. Find an open place to do yoga as deep breathing and relaxation are part of it.

Cool-down Exercises

As you start your exercise program with warm-up exercises, end it with some cool-down exercises. These exercises are to lower your heart rate and give your muscle little relaxation. Once done with your regular workout program, do some basic stretching to relax your muscles and joints. In Yoga, there is a relaxation technique called autosuggestion, and an asana called savasana as part of these exercises. And to recover and replenish, drink a glass of water and eat a banana after your cool-down exercises.

"If you don't find time for exercise now,
you will have to find time for illness later."

—*Wayne Pickering*

Five best ways to include an exercise in your lifestyle

Body weight exercises

For doing body weight exercises neither you need any equipment nor you need more time. 15-20 minutes of a vigorous body weight exercise is enough to build muscle and protect the muscle loss. Wear your sports suit, play your favourite music and get ready for some challenges. Just start with some joint rotations, jumping jack and toe-touch as warm-up before moving to the body weight exercises. Choose any 5-6 exercises from the list and start doing, giving little break in between.

Push ups	Squats	Planks
Burpees	Lunges	Crunches
Mountain Climber	Squat jumps	Double leg lifts
Superman	Wall sits	Russian Twist

Yoga

As a Yoga practitioner and trainer, I always recommend everyone to do yoga, at least 20-30 minutes, few days a week. Yoga asanas are easy to practice and you can do them anywhere. You just need your sports suit and a yoga mat. Yes, it is important to practice yoga in open air as it involves lots of breathing practices. Before practicing at home, try to learn the basics of yoga from a professional trainer.

Walking/Running/Cycling/Stair climbing

The simplest and easiest option for you to start is walking. Wear your track suits and sport shoe and get ready for a walk. You can do it, early morning, post lunch, or even after your daily job. You can add running to your daily lifestyle, it is just higher version of walking. Running burns more calories than walking but if you have any injuries, it's better to walk instead of running. Another easy option can be cycling. Buy an indoor cycle and do cycling while enjoying your favourite TV shows or match. You can buy a cycle to commute to your office. Many people are doing this for keeping environment clean and burn calories. And the last option in this category is you can use the stairs in your apartment to do an incline walk. In inclined walk, you can burn more calories than the normal walk as it is against the gravity.

Your favourite childhood sport

This is an interesting way to add physical activity into your lifestyle. I am sure; everyone has a few childhood games in their memory whether it's indoor or outdoor. However, here I am talking about an outdoor game that you enjoyed most in your childhood. For me, it's cricket. In India, most of the people enjoyed cricket in their childhood because of the popularity of this game. The problem is, once we left our hometown for studies or job, we ignored it. Now, it's the time to find a group and again become a child with your favourite game. It is beneficial for both of our body and mind. By adding childhood sports into our lifestyle, you'll get regular physical activity and you'll become stress free. If not possible every day because of your busy life, try to play the game at least once or twice a week over a weekend or early morning. Now, call your friends, make a group, find a ground and decide the day to start the game. Just do it today, you will never regret for this decision.

NEAT

NEAT stands for Non-Exercise Activity Thermogenesis. In plain English, this means: Be more active! "Sitting is the new smoking"–sitting kills more people than smoking. In this desktop lifestyle, it's really challenging to be more active. To be healthy and fit, find some way to ditch this dangerous sedentary lifestyle. Walk more often. Use a basket instead of a trolley at the supermarket (unless you've got a truck-load of stuff to buy). Skip the lift and take the stairs. Do your household chores. Stand while making a phone call. Walk your dog. And play more games. Just be more active.

Exercise and Total Energy Expenditure (TEE)

There is a misunderstanding that we burn calories only in exercise. Yes, exercise or physical activity plays a vital role in TEE and weight management. For maintaining our normal weight, understand first the energy balance.

Energy Balance:

Energy Intake = Energy Expenditure

A. Positive Energy Balance:

Energy Intake > Energy Expenditure; here, weight is gained and fat stores are increased.

B. Negative Energy Balance:

Energy Intake < Energy Expenditure; weight is lost and fat stores are burned.

It's easy to understand the Energy Intake, which is mainly through our food. Let's understand the most confusing part, Energy expenditure, TEE.

$$\textbf{TEE = BMR + TEF + NEAT + EPOC + Exercise}$$

TEE: Total Energy Expenditure

BMR: Basal Metabolic Rate

TEF: Thermic Effect of Food

NEAT: Non-Exercise activity thermogenesis

EPOC: Excess post-exercise oxygen consumption

BMR: It stands for *Basal Metabolic Rate or Resting Metabolic Rate* (RMR). It's the energy required for maintaining all bodily functions such as respiration, blood circulation, body temperature regulation, maintaining all vital organs, and brain functions.

- Body's largest user of energy.

- Minimum amount of calorie necessary for the body to maintain normal functions (60 to 70% of total energy)

- Depends on many factors such as

  - Genetics

  - Gender (Men > Women)

  - Age (Drops with age)

  - Weight (Increases with Muscle mass)

  - Height (Increases with Height)

  - Diet

  - Body temperature and external temperature

TEF: It stands for *Thermic Effect of Food.* It's the energy used for food digestion and absorption. Carbs are easily absorbed and take very little energy to digest where Proteins are harder to process and take more energy. That's why, fitness experts recommend eating more protein if your goal is to lose weight. TEF accounts for about 10% of total energy burned.

NEAT: It stands for *Non-Exercise Activity Thermogenesis.* It's the energy used in an activity other than sleeping, eating and exercise. It includes walking, shopping, gardening, cooking, etc.

EPOC: It stands for *Excessive Post Oxygen Consumption.* It's the energy used in cellular repair and muscle recovery after exercise. The high intensity creates the after burn effect (aka EPOC)which causes your body to continue to burn more calories for up to 24-30 hours after your workout is over.The EPOC effect is good, but to make it great, you've got to combine it with NEAT.

Exercise: It is the most variable component of TEE. It's completely depended upon our active lifestyle and physical activity level.

From the above five components of TEE, you have less control over BMR and TEF. However, you have more control over the other three. By following a regular exercise program whether it's a gym session or yoga practice or 30 minutes of cardio, you can burn more calories and being more active throughout the day you can increase the effect of EPOC and NEAT. Keeping this in mind, let's move to one of the frequently asked questions on exercise…

How much exercise do we need?

American Health Association (AHA) and many fitness experts recommend 150 minutes of moderate activity or 75 minutes of high intensity exercise per week. However, considering our current sedentary lifestyle, it's a best practice to do 30 to 45 minutes of exercise daily to be fit and energetic. In my 4 years of research and interviews with many health experts, what I found is, you should divide your exercise program into two parts.

Your Daily Exercise Session

This is your 60 to 90 minutes of workout session depending upon your fitness goal and busy schedule. You can do many different workouts and activities in this exercise session. You can join a Gym for bodybuilding, or can join a yoga class or even can attend a dance or Zumba class. You should keep at least 5 sessions every week to be fit and healthy. You can easily burn the extra calories and reduce the store fat by doing this much exercise.

The Magic Number

It's not enough for your body if you just do a 1 hour of exercise in the morning or evening and throughout the day live a sedentary lifestyle. As you know, "Sitting is the new smoking", you have to be more active and live an active lifestyle. Now, How to define the active lifestyle? The researchers made it easy for us; active lifestyle means just 10,000 steps a day.

Throughout the day you need to achieve the magic number, 10,000 steps. That means, move more and sit less. Ditch the sedentary lifestyle. It seems like a huge but it's easy to achieve this target. You just need to walk 5 miles (8 km) every day. Don't sit for longer hours in an office or home and don't use the lift at office and home. Use the pulsing technique at your work, means work in a cycle. After working for 50 to 60 minutes, take a walking break for 10 to 15 minutes. It will make you fit and increase your productivity. If you achieve the magic number, you will burn about 400 to 500 calories a day, which means you can lose one pound (3500 calories) every week.

How to Choose the right and best exercise for you

"It's going to be a journey;
it's not a sprint to get in shape."

—Kerri Walsh Jennings

Gym membership is one of the top money wasters in the world. People join gyms with excitement after the New Year resolution or watching their favourite celebrity in the movie or documentary. As my friend said it, "it's not January, but Gym-uary!" It's not about just start a fitness program, it's about the consistency. One of the major reason I found to quit any fitness program is boredom. People get bored with the particular exercise session or some diet plan, so, they quit. It is important to select the right exercise pattern for you and make it a part of your lifestyle.

Tips for choosing best exercise pattern

Try different exercises

There are many types of exercises starting from very ancient yoga to modern gym. Try different exercises before choosing the best one for you. You can try cardio exercises in the gym or you just prefer to walking and running in the field. Also you can join a gym to do weight exercises or you can try various body weight exercises like Push-ups, squats, planks, etc.You can also try some other flexibility exercises like Yoga. By trying different exercises, you can find the best exercise which you can do, week-in and week-out.

Choose the exercise that you enjoy most

After trying many exercises, choose those exercises you enjoy most. Check your goal and according to that, choose the best one. Now, it's easy to find various exercises at one place or in a single gym or health club. After doing a month of gym session, I found yoga in my gym. I like it so much that I become a regular practitioner first and then, become a yoga trainer. Apart from yoga, I love to go for a long walk and enjoy stair climbing.You can try weight training, calisthenics, yoga, walking/running, stair climbing, cycling, swimming, or any dance exercises like aerobic or Zumba and then choose the exercise that you like.

Add multiple exercises into your routine

One of the easiest ways to avoid the boredom in exercise is adding different exercises into your routine. I love to do yoga, however sometimes our mind want little different. Instead of going against our mind, I try Tabata- a bodyweight exercise series with music and the very next day, back to yoga series. You should try to add multiple exercises into your routine from different categories. Some muscle or weight training exercises, some cardio exercise and some flexibility exercises. And yes, don't forget to play your childhood sports.

Set up a low cost home gym

A home gym has a lot of benefits. In our so called busy life, sometimes it's difficult to find time for exercise or go to gym. By setting up a low cost home gym, you can follow your workout program even on the busiest day. Because it's open 24*7 and require no time to reach. Here, I am not talking about having all the equipment in your home gym, but the necessary one. In my home gym, I have a pair of dumbbells and kettle bells for strength training, two yoga mats for my yoga practice, and a cycle for cardio. So, think little on this, just go and invest this little money and build your own temple.

Find an exercise partner

By finding a good friendly partner, you can make your exercises fun. The gym and health club can be a boring place, doing the same workouts everyday may not be ideal, having a friend as your workout partner will make the exercising more enjoyable. Sometimes you are feeling lazy to do a workout or you are feeling tired and want to skip the workout, on these off days, having an exercise partner will make you more accountable and consistent. Also, you can learn more about the subject and challenge each other to grow in performance as someone says, "Don't go together, but grow together".

Hire a personal trainer

If you are new to a workout, it is better to hire a good professional trainer and learn proper techniques from him. There is a greater chance of injuries if you'll not follow the proper form and technique. A personal trainer can guide you with all the basics and fundamentals of the workouts. He can understand your goal and guide you with the perfect exercise plan or any changes you require throughout the program. A trainer is a great resource with knowledge on different areas and has a network with other specialists in the areas of nutrition, body massages, and more.

Exercise and Sweating

"Sweat is just FAT crying, make it rain."

—Anonymous

This is a very basic and common question but it's important to know the benefits of sweating. We have about

4 million sweat glands that excrete a mixture of water, salt, amino acids, proteins, and other substances. The main compositions of sweat are sodium, potassium, calcium, magnesium, copper, iron, chromium, urea (a by-product of protein), and lactic acid. Let's discuss some benefits of sweating from exercise.

A Thermo regulator (Cooling down)

When you sweat, it's like a mini air conditioner. It helps you regulate your internal temperature. When the sweat glands release sweat onto your skin, it'll evaporate cooling your skin and the blood underneath. This will help to bring down your bodies rising internal temperature.

A Natural Detox

Research shows that sweating is your body's way of releasing natural and unnatural toxins from your system. Toxins like bad cholesterol, excess sodium, and urea. In our modern diet, we are taking way more sodium than our body require and the excess of sodium results into high blood pressure, kidney stones, and also loss of calcium in the body. You can eliminate on average 900 mg of sodium every single hour of sweating from exercise.A study of Chinese residents found that those who exercised more had fewer toxins in their body and that the elimination of heavy metals was more concentrated in sweat than urine. You need to sweat every single day through various exercises to eliminate these harmful toxins out from your body.

Makes you happier

When you sweat from exercise, your body releases happy hormone endorphins. It is a natural mood enhancer. So, if you are feeling little down, you can try adding exercise into your routine and sweat to release this mood enhancing hormone which can make you healthier and happier person.

Lower stress hormones

Sympathetic nervous system activates by the hormone Cortisol, 'flight-or-fight' hormone. However Parasympathetic nervous system leads to rest and relaxation. Sweating activates the parasympathetic response in the body that allows us to relax and recover. Sweating through exercise helps to boost our happy hormones and reduce the stress hormones and cortisol.

Healthier looking skin

Because of the environmental and internal toxins, our sweat glands fill with the gunk which can cause skin irritation and acne. Sweating is one of the best ways, apart from good hygiene, to remove that entire gunk. That's why you see your favourite celebrities hit gym every day and sweats a lot. So, why so late, go do some exercise and clear up the skin.

Lower risk of kidney stones

Now, incidence of kidney stones is very common. Researchers at the University of Washington found the benefit of sweating through consistent exercise reduces this risk. Excess sodium and calcium can form kidney stones over time however sweating eliminates the excess sodium and directs calcium to our bones.

2X WORKOUT Model

*"If you capsuled all the benefits of exercise,
it will be one of the high selling and costlier drug."*

—AD

Towards the end of 2017, while searching on Google on New Year resolutions, I found this new workout model. With no delay, I started researching more on this and its major benefits. It's a revelation for me after knowing how this simple workout model can help in better decision making and remove stress and anxiety from our life. Hence, I added this new model to my New Year resolution for 2018 and made it part of my lifestyle.

In this workout model, you need to divide your exercise program into two parts.

1. **Early Morning Workout:**- Do this first thing in the morning. As soon as you wake up in the morning, do some exercise for at least 15-20 minutes. You can do some quick body weight exercises, go for a brisk walking or do some basic stretching. The idea behind is, to give your body a wake-up call. It improves the blood circulation and secretes many happy hormones in the body. Research says,

those who exercise in the morning, they are better decision makers in their life.

2. **Post job Evening Workout:** -Try to do after your daily job or work. Once you back from your job, you just need to a little workout for at least 15-20 minutes. You can go for a run, or just walk in the garden while talking with your friends or you can just hit the gym to sweat a bit. Throughout the day, you face many challenges and conflict of thoughts with your job and life, results into stress and anxiety. This quick workout program helps you to release the stress and anxiety by secreting some happy hormones like serotonin and endorphins. It helps you to have a better relationship with family and better sleep.

Anti-Gravity Exercises

Anti-gravity exercise is aerobic and slightly anaerobic exercise which involves repeated and continuous movement of large muscle groups like core and leg muscles. During these exercises, the need of glucose increases at a faster pace. Because of this, blood glucose gets pulled into the muscle cells without the need of insulin. If you do just for 10-15 of these exercises, you will see an instant blood sugar down. These exercises are a must for diabetes reversal. The best ways to incorporate these anti-gravity exercises in your lifestyle are,

- **Stair Climbing:** Just start with 200-300 steps daily. Avoid this exercise, if you have knee pain. Use the stairs instead of the lift or escalator at home, office and malls.

- **Body Movements:** Move your hands and legs against the gravity. This is a good option for old-age people or people having knee-pain.

- **Trekking:** This perfectly combines antigravity exercise with fresh air & sunlight. Find a nearest hill and go for 2-3 hours or even a fullday trekking once in a week.

- **Inclined Walking:** Set your treadmill in inclined option and walk for 20-30 minutes, taking a rest in between.

Give yourself a challenge

> *"Challenge yourself; it's the only path which leads to growth."*
>
> **—Morgan Freeman**

Taking a decision or resolution to do exercise is easy but to maintain it and doing it consistently is the most challenging part. You read this book and understand the importance of health and exercise. You decide and promise to yourself that you will do exercise every single day. I have an ample amount of faith and believe on you and your decision; however I have a little doubt on your mind. There is a great chance, it will bored after some days and force you to quit the program. That's why I always add the power of challenge with my decision.

Challenge makes you out of your comfort zone. It adds extra fuel to your goal and aim. Give yourself a challenge now; it can make exercise more enjoyable.When I started doing exercise, I gave myself a challenge to do 50 push ups in a go and a 90 day no miss workout session. This simple challenge makes me not only healthy but also more confident in my life. It's even better if you share your challenge with your family and friends; just ask them to remind you time to time. I am sure, they are best in that. In India, everyone has an expertise in giving free advice to others. You can also use some online applications for this; there are many applications available there. Take advantage of that and start today with your challenges.

Some Challenges to start with

1. Number of push ups in a single set/ Your Plank duration

2. Number of days not to miss a workout, follow the schedule

3. Register yourself for a marathon

4. Go for a fix BMI or Body fat%

5. Go for a six-pack abs

6. 54 or 108 rounds of sun salutation in a go

7. Achieving the magic number–10,000 steps every single day

Few More Exercises You Should Know

"I love exercise but I find it boring doing the same thing all the time, so I fluctuate between going to the gym, doing Pilates and taking dance lessons."

—Twiggy

Now, after reading over 10 pages on exercise, I presumed that you have already added exercise into your lifestyle and also, the right pattern of it. As you know, all new things excite us for first few days and later, we feel boredom with the same thing. Here, it's my responsibility to give you few more exercises to make your journey not only enjoyable but also longer. I tried these exercises and definitely it will give you some new experiences.

1. HIIT & TABATA
2. Advance Yoga.
3. Functional Training
4. Ido Portal Method
5. Dancercise
6. Isometrics & Plyometric
7. Walking, Running and Marathons
8. Calisthenics

My Home Gym - A pair of Dumbbell, Kettle bell and Yoga mat

*"For Exercise, you don't need any equipment.
You just need a strong willpower."*

—AD

After my first gym membership expired, I did this experiment. To save my commute time in the morning, I set up a home Gym. And the most important things came to my mind is the space and budget. For space, I rearranged my drawing room, and the problem solved over one weekend. For Money, I added a little extra money with my gym membership renewal fees. In the very next weekend, I went to decathlon and brought 2 pair of dumbbells, 1 pair of kettle bells, 2 yoga mat and some gloves with a push up stand. As the cycle for cardio was out of my budget, I checked that online for any resellers. Apart from equipment, I ordered some motivational postures and air-filtering plants to make my temple complete. And within a week, I setup my cute and sweet home gym with all necessary equipment for strength training, cardio, and flexibility. Here, some lessons I learned from my home gym and experiment.

1. It saves time in a busy day

2. 24 * 7 Open for you

> 3. Yes, little boring if you don't like Exercise
>
> 4. One of the best investments
>
> 5. Kettle bells are awesome

Revise Notes

- Exercise is a miracle drug because of its many benefits on body and mind. Ditch all the excuses for not doing and start doing exercise from today.

- There are five types of exercises–warm up, strength training, cardio, and flexibility and cool down. Try the different exercises like Yoga, Body weight exercises, running or trekking.

- TEE = BMR + TEF + NEAT + EPOC + Exercise

- You need to exercise at least 1 hour daily and throughout the day try to be active and cover 10,000 steps.

- Choose the right and best exercise for you to avoid the boredom. Sweat more. Sometimes challenge yourself by registering an upcoming marathon or a 108 sun-salutations.

- Do 2X workouts at least 5 days a week.

To know more on Exercise, check the videos on youtube. com/alokdwibedy.

Action Exercise

1. What are the exercises you are doing right now? Or planning to start with?

2. What do you prefer, morning or evening workout?

3. Write the number of steps for the upcoming week.

4. What are the challenges you set for next 5 week?

5. What is your childhood game? And when did you play the game last time?

TWO

NUTRITION

"We are digging our graves with our teeth."

—Thomas Moffett

"Our food should be our medicine and our medicine should be our food."

—Hippocrates

If I would be the health minister, then the very first course I will introduce in school level curriculum is this–"knowing the importance of nutrition". The first thing Barack Obama did after becoming the president of America to improve the healthcare system is that he started working on prevention diseases and the role of nutritional awareness in it. Lack of proper knowledge on nutrition is one of the major reasons behind many lifestyle diseases. I know the importance of this when I started doing exercise with no major changes in my diet. And because of this, I felt tired in the office and after the office. Then, I started learning and researching on this beautiful life changing topic. I read some awesome books and joined some online courses on health and nutrition. Later, I loved this subject so much that I became a Fitness Nutrition Coach. The most important experience I have in this 3 years' journey is, "Nutrition is one of the most confusing subjects in this health and wellness industry for lack of proper knowledge." And as you know, there is a huge difference between information and knowledge. Everyone is rich in information but very poor in knowledge. So, let's dive into the most confusing world of nutrition to know some beautiful concepts from my knowledge and experiments.

Let's learn it...

DIET vs. LIFESTYLE

"It's not a short term diet. It's a long-term lifestyle change."

—AD

When we are serious about our excess weight and want to go for fitness routine, the first thing comes to our mind is dieting. Then, we look for a very healthy and strict diet with low carbohydrates and a high protein (FAD diet). But do we know that 90% of these dieting fail in the long run? How many days will you eat the same routine and boring food? To make it permanent and longer, go for few healthy lifestyle changes and enjoy your health and fitness.

Dieting is temporary

If dieting works, then think, why there are so many varieties of diets available. It's because dieting is temporary and not a particular diet last for a longer period. The only thing last is a healthy lifestyle changes that is made with proper awareness and according to your health goal. Yes, sometimes dieting is important for a shorter period in case of any competition, or any fitness target to achieve in the next two to three months. For example, any bodybuilding competition, or any life event like marriages, or any defence interview. If dieting works, then only one diet plan is enough to make you fit not so many kinds of diet like keto diet, paleo diet, Mediterranean diet, vegan diet, juice diet, Atkins diet, dash diet and list goes on. Important point to note here is no diet will work unless you work on your lifestyle.

"Only Humans goes on a diet and all other species has a diet. It's time to find our natural diet – The Human Diet."

—AD

Why I became a Lifestyle coach

After coming back from Hospital, I started learning a lot on Nutrition. And because of lots of doubts and confusion, I did a nutrition course and became a fitness nutritionist. As a nutritionist, I got to know all the basics and fundamentals of diet and nutrition. Immediately after that, I started giving diet to my friends, colleagues and some clients. However, after watching their progress and outcome, I didn't believe on dieting anymore and started researching on the failure of dieting in the long term and found that dieting is temporary. Then, I read some books and research papers on lifestyle and weight management. I joined a course on Lifestyle coaching and in 20 weeks of analysis and experiment, I became a Lifestyle Coach. Now, I am helping my clients with the new formulae–Lifestyle Changes, a permanent health and weight management technique.

Different types of Diets

In my years of research on health and nutrition, I came across different types of diets from my clients and colleagues,

1. **Keto Diet:** It is a short-term low carb, high-fat diet that focuses on weight loss: 70% Fat, 25% Protein, and 5% Carbs.

2. **Paleo Diet:** A Paleo diet includes meats, seafood, vegetables, low-sugar fruits, most nuts, and healthy oils. It strictly eliminates grains, legumes, dairy, sugars, potatoes, peanuts, vegetable / hydrogenated oils, and all processed foods.

3. **Mediterranean Diet:** It is high in fruits, vegetables, legumes, grains, nuts, seeds, fish, and unsaturated fat like olive oil. It also includes a limited amount of dairy products and meat.

4. **Vegan Diet:** It is a complete plant-based diet and avoids any foods that come from an animal. This includes meats, seafood, dairy, eggs, and honey.

5. **Atkins Diet:** It is another fad diet which includes fat and protein but low in carbohydrate. The focus is to lose weight and improve health.

6. **DASH Diet:** DASH stands for Dietary Approaches to Stop Hypertension. It includes fruits, vegetables and low fat dairy products.

Common Lifestyle changes

Lifestyle is the new diet and medicine. We will discuss a lot on this powerful drug throughout the book but for now, let's check on some basic lifestyle changes require irrespective of your health goal.

1. **Exercise Regularly:** Ditch the sedentary lifestyle. Live an active lifestyle.

2. **Eat a Healthy Diet:** Avoid highly processed food. Add more nutritious food into your diet.

3. **Practice Deep Breathing:** Practice pranayama or few deep breaths daily.

4. **Drink Plenty of Water:** Not only mineral water. But have water from the fruits, vegetables, electrolytes and sprouts.

5. **Practice Meditation:** Mindfulness and Meditation is the key to have a peaceful mind.

6. **Relax and Have Fun:** Relaxation is nature's way of recharging our body and mind.

7. **Maintain a Healthy weight:** Check your BMI and BF%. Make your Belly flat.

8. **Have some Sunshine Daily:** Have sunshine for vitamin D and melatonin hormone especially in the morning hours.

> 9. **Play some Game:** It can be your favourite childhood game or any mental activity. Play and Relax.
>
> 10. **Have Great Hobbies:** Reading books, Dance, Music, Bodybuilding, Spirituality or Public speaking.

Processed vs. Unprocessed Food

For lifestyle changes, the most challenging one is changing our eating habit and do some changes to our regular diet. Let's make it simple now. Hey, my dear reader, please follow these two things–it will literally change your life.

> *"Our walls and ceiling of our kitchens have*
> *more nutrients than our food plate."*

1. **Man-made Vs. Nature-made:** Nature provides us all the essential nutrients in the natural form of food. We then cooked or processed it and make it a calorie dense food. Take the example of Cooked Vegetables or Fruit Juices with added sugar or Tea/Coffee with dairy and sugar.

2. **In-the-Plant vs. Inside-the-Plant:** Here the first plant is nature or trees while the latter one is a factory. See, Banana is coming from a banana tree but banana chips are coming from the factory with lots of salt and trans-fat. Similarly, tomato is

coming from the tomato plant but tomato sauce is coming from the factory with lots of added sugar, salts, chemicals, and preservatives. Try to have more and more foods in the natural form from the nature or a little process of cooking.

Processed food has more sugar, salt, chemicals, preservatives and high in trans-fat. It includes any packaged foods and highly cooked foods. Delete the processed foods from your diet and have a lot of unprocessed food.

Eat your Rainbow

The next lifestyle change I recommend to my clients is to add fruits and vegetables of different colours in their diets. Fruits and Vegetables are high in vitamins, minerals, fiber and unique disease fighting chemicals called phytochemicals. These phytochemicals gives fruits and vegetables their respective colours.

Take these 4 Types of Veggies Daily

This one lifestyle change that helped me to gain back my health and it will help you too. We know vegetables are rich in micronutrients, fiber, phytochemicals and anti-oxidants. But the most important thing to know about vegetables is they are our internal organ's best friends.

1. Type-1: *Colourful Peppers*

    There are two main foods for Cancer cells in our body–Glucose and Glutamine. You can easily stop the Glucose part by removing all the simple carbohydrates. But it's challenging for you to avoid glutamine as it is ubiquitous. Nature gives you a way to inhibit glutamine through these powerful peppers. Add fresh colourful peppers into your diet to control the cancer food, glutamine.

2. Type-2: *Cruciferous Vegetables*

   Cruciferous vegetables are superfoods for your liver. The major function of the liver is detoxification, and it happens in two phases. In the phase one, it protects from a wide variety of toxic chemicals and in phase two, through conjugation, it makes the toxins water-soluble to ease the elimination. Cruciferous vegetables like broccoli, cabbage, cauliflower enhance the phase two detoxification. Apart from the detoxification, Broccoli is one of the best sources of vegetable protein and low in calorie.

3. Type-3: *Green Leafy Vegetables*

   Green leafy vegetables are rich in micronutrients. Excess sodium is harmful for your body. It leads to weight gain and hypertension. Potassium helps your kidneys get rid of more sodium through your urine. And these leafy greens spinach, Celery, Wheatgrass, Beet leaves, Mustard greens are rich in potassium. Another key element here is Chlorophyll. The structure of Chlorophyll and

Haemoglobin are quiet same. That's why wheatgrass juice is known as "green blood" as it is loaded with chlorophyll.

4. Type-4: *Salad Family*

    Salad family vegetable means the raw vegetables you should eat just before your major meals. It includes cucumber, carrot, tomato, beet, cabbage, lettuce, radish or capsicums. Gut is your second brain and prebiotics are the best foods for your healthy gut microbiomes. These raw vegetables are a great source of prebiotics. It helps in digestion and elimination process.

Delete these two poisons–Refined Sugar and Refined Oil

In our "5 fact fitness" program and retreat, I asked the participants to delete few things immediately from the kitchen. Refined sugar and refined oil are always on the top of the list. Always remember, processed foods are always comes with the "-extra", extra calories, extra chemicals, extra preservatives, extra fat etc. Refined sugar and oil are highly processed and have very few nutrients. These are calorie-dense foods.

Sugar is the new Nicotine

There is one truth the processed food industry not telling you is–"These foods will make you addictive because of their nature". The refined sugar (white sugar, white rice, and white flour) in your kitchen is the main reason behind many health problems in your life starting from lifestyle diseases like diabetes, cancer to common problems like digestion and dental diseases. In India, we use it in many food items like tea, coffee, sweets, and bakery items to the junk foods. You will be surprised to know that the white colour of sugar is not a natural colour, it is for bleaching. Through highly processed method, there are no nutritional contents in it and it spikes the blood sugar immediately.

"Be careful while checking the ingredients,
there are at least 61 different names for sugar.
Stay away from the processed food."

—AD

Healthy substitutes are:

White Sugar: Natural sweeteners like natural honey or raw Jaggery.

White Rice: Complex carb like Oats, Brown rice, Dalia, or Quinoa.

White Flour: Multi-grain Flour.

Refine Oil–Fat that Kill

The most dangerous fat for our body is Trans Fat. These refined oils when exposed to a little heat transformed into trans-fat. This leads to high cholesterol, blockage arteries, blood pressures and heart related diseases. Refined oil extraction involves high supply of heat to extract maximum oils out of seeds. On top of this, to extract more oil, they use chemicals and solvents. Here, oils come with fewer nutrients and added chemicals and toxics.

Healthy substitutes are Pure Home-made Desi Ghee or Traditional Wood Churner oil.

The traditional method of wood pressing or cold pressing doesn't involve any external heat. They crushed the seeds in the wooden axis. There are no added chemicals in the oil. Although there is less production of oils in this process, they are much healthier than the modern day refined oil.

Calorie Dense Vs. Nutrient Dense

"Do we need to count the Calories?" a common question asked by many of my clients. And the answer is a big 'NO' if your goal is to be fit and healthy. Counting calories of the diet or meal is a must if your goals to take part in any bodybuilding competition or you are a sports person or a celebrity who signed a contract for the next project for a certain physique. To be fit and healthy, what important is to know the nutrients in the particular food. Let me explain this with an example. Suppose you need to choose in between a glass of soft drinks and a bowl of papaya, which one you choose? If you want to know the calorie, then both have same, 150 calories. But the glass of soft drinks have only one nutrient that is simple carbohydrates (sugars) while the bowl of papaya have many nutrients like vitamins, minerals, digestive enzymes, phytonutrients, and fiber. So, choose food as per their nutrients density that means fewer calories but more nutrients. Raw foods like fruits, vegetables, sprouts and micro or baby greens have more nutrient density than the cooked and processed food.

Avoid the empty calories

Our body never understand the difference between an apple and a potato, what it understands is the nutrients in the particular food and it functions according to it. Try to avoid the calorie-dense foods that are high in calories and empty in nutrients. That's why it called Empty calories. All the simple carbohydrates like refined sugar, refined flour, packaged food items like biscuits, breads comes under this category. It just spike your blood sugar immediately and to control that the beta cells of your pancreas secrets the hormone, insulin. If it happens frequently, then your cells and organs of your body become resistance to the insulin and we called it "Insulin Resistance". And the very next step is Type-II Diabetes. India is on top of the list having several Diabetes patients and known as "Diabetes Capital of the World". To prevent this lifestyle disease, the simple formula is removing these empty calories.

Know the basic nutrients

The very first step towards a healthy living is having a better awareness of all the essential nutrients for your body. Essential nutrients are those that the body can't make it and you must take it from your food. To have a disease-free and healthy life, you must take all the essential nutrients in your diet. We broadly classify them into two categories–Macronutrients and Micronutrients.

(A) Macronutrients

As the name suggest, your body need these nutrients in larger amount. These nutrients build your body and provide the energy. These include Carbohydrate, Protein and Fat.

CARBS: Carbs are the body's main and first source of energy. Carbs break down into glucose, which is used for energy. The unused carbs also stored in the liver and other body parts as fat for later use (Carbs → Glycogen → Fat). The main sources are fruits, vegetables, grains, sugar, milk and yoghurt. 1 gram of carb = 4 calories. You should consume 30-40% of your total calories from carbs. But it depends on your current fitness goal.

PROTEIN: Protein is not for energy but for maintenance. It is essential for growth, tissue repair, preserving lean muscle, and producing hormones and enzymes. Protein from food converts into amino acids and from these amino acids body prepares its own proteins. The main sources are animal products, lentils, nuts and seeds. 1 gram of protein = 4 calories.

You should consume 25-35% of your total calories from protein.

FAT: Fats are the secondary source of energy. It is essential for joints, tissue and hormone production. Fats are also essential for absorbing the fat-soluble vitamins–Vitamin A, D, E, and K. If fats consumed are not burned then they're stored as body fat. The main sources are–fatty fishes, coconut oil, olive oil, Ghee, nuts and seeds. 1 gram of fat = 9 calories. You should consume 10-25% of your total calories from healthy fat (PUFA).

(B) Micronutrients

Unlike macronutrients, your body need these nutrients in smaller amounts. Smaller doesn't mean unimportant. Deficiencies in these nutrients can lead to major health problems. Micronutrients include vitamins and minerals. It requires vitamins and minerals in little amount to perform many important roles in our body, boosting our immune system, strengthening our bones, converting food into energy and repairing the cellular damage.

(a) Vitamin

(b) Mineral

(c) Antioxidant

VITAMIN: Vitamins are of two types, water soluble & fat soluble. Water-soluble vitamins are Vitamin B & C. These vitamins dissolve in water and easily pass out of the body as waste. So, you need frequent supply of these vitamins. Fat-soluble vitamins are Vitamin A, D, and E & K. These are absorbed with the help of fat. Body can store these vitamins. Fruits, vegetables, sprouts, greens, nuts and seeds are rich in vitamins.

MINERAL: Minerals do many functions in the body like supporting immune system, preventing deficiency and building strong bones and teeth. There are two types of minerals–macro minerals and trace minerals. Body needs larger amounts of macro minerals than trace minerals. The macro minerals include calcium, phosphorous, magnesium, sodium, potassium, chloride, iron and zinc. Foods high in essential minerals are nuts, beans, leafy greens, seeds, mushrooms and whole grains.

ANTIOXIDANTS: Antioxidants can stabilize or deactivate free radicals before they can attack healthy cells. An antioxidant can be a vitamin, mineral or phytochemical. Examples of dietary antioxidants include beta-carotene, lycopene, and vitamin A, C and E. They are naturally present in vegetables, fruits, whole grains, lentils, nuts and seeds.

Complex Carbs—Your Gut's friend

Carbohydrates comprises of three components: fiber, starch, and sugar. Fiber and starch are complex carbs, while sugar is a simple carb. Complex carbohydrates are derived from plants that contain both starch and dietary fiber. This includes vegetables, potatoes, dried beans, grains and fruits. Animal products contain little, if any carbohydrates. Fiber is your gut's best friend.

The main role of Fiber is to keep the digestive system healthy. We need 25-35 grams of fiber per day. Fiber is mainly complex carbohydrate. As our foods are energy dense, they are packed with simple carbohydrate which misses this important Fiber. Our Gut bugs love plant-based fibre.

Benefits of High-Fiber Diet:

1. Normalizes Bowel movement

2. Lowers cholesterol levels

3. Control Blood sugar levels

4. Maintain a healthy weight

The Real Carbs

Best Food Sources for Carbohydrate—As carbohydrates have the word 'hydrates' in it, choose the carbs that have water in it like fruits and vegetables. Hence, Raw Fruits &Vegetables are real carb as they are full in fiber. Apart from these, you can have whole grains and beans.

The Protein Game

Protein is a macronutrient, used for building, maintaining and repairing muscle, skin and blood (supplies very little energy to the body). Our body make its own proteins and it needs all the amino acids in the amino acid pool. Protein, as food, provides the amino acids that body needs to synthesize its own proteins.

Amino Acids:

There are two types of amino acids–Essential and Non-essential.

1. *Essential Amino acid*: Essential amino acids are those amino acids that our body cannot synthesize. We must therefore obtain essential amino acids from our diet. As traditionally defined, the essential amino acids are Histidine, Isoleucine, Leucine, Lysine, Methionine, Phenylalanine, Threonine, Tryptophan, and Valine.

2. *Non-essential Amino acid*: Nonessential amino acids are those that the body can manufacture itself. It is therefore unnecessary to get these amino acids from the diet. As traditionally defined, the nonessential amino acids include Glutamate, Alanine, Aspartate, Glutamine, Arginine, Proline, Serine, Tyrosine, Cysteine, Taurine, and Glycine. But on certain conditions, our body can't make all the amino acids. For example, when a person is exposed to large

amounts of environmental toxins and pollutants, the amount of glycine (a non-essential amino acid) made by the body may be far from adequate. It's better if we call these nonessential amino acids as "conditionally essential" and also considered these while thinking about the nourishment.

Best Food Sources for Protein:

When it comes to food sources for protein, always focus on quality over quantity. Non-veg sources are complete protein as these foods have all the essential amino acids but it comes with cholesterol and zero fiber. Veg sources are incomplete, as a single veg food except Soya doesn't have all the essential amino acids. Veg source of protein are quality protein for its nutrient density and zero cholesterol. Apart from that, you can make it complete by mixing the grains with lentils. In different part of India, you will find this combination like 'Dal + Rice', 'Rajma + Chawal', 'Sambhar + Rice', Waran + Bhat'.

Fat is NOT the Enemy—Choose healthy fats

Few decades ago, fat was harmful food for our body. Now, the experts recommend a good amount of fat in our daily diet. Why it happened? The answer is not all fats are harmful but few really are. There are 4 types of fats,

1. *Saturated Fat (SaFa):* The main sources of these fats are, refined cooking oil, meat and meat products,

sugar, refined flour. A minimum amount of these fats in your diet is okay but try to reduce as much as possible.

2. *Monounsaturated Fat (MuFa):* The other name of this fat is "Omega-9". And it's non-essential. Our body can make these fats itself. No need to take these fats in the form of food.

3. *Polyunsaturated Fat (PuFa):* Famously known as "Omega 3 & 6". It's called the essential fatty acid. We have to take these fats in the form of food, our body can't make it. The most important thing to take care here is the ratio of omega 6 to omega 3.The ideal ratio should be 2:1 or max 4:1. But because of lack of omega 3 in our diet, the real ratio sometime exceeds 10:1 or even 20:1. Omega 6 is easily available in the form of processed cooking oil like sunflower oil or safflower oil and dairy products. Add at least a few good sources of omega-3 in your diet like pure desi ghee, coconut, olive oil, nuts and seeds especially flax seed.

4. *Trans-fat:* The most dangerous fat and main reason behind obesity, high cholesterol, blockage artery, and heart attacks. Delete these fats from your diet. The best way to do that is to reduce or remove all the processed and packaged food from your diet. Highly cooked food items are rich in trans-fat.

Good or Bad Cholesterol

"There is no cholesterol in plants. All animals produce their own cholesterol."

Cholesterol is a fat and is required in the production of hormones like oestrogen, progesterone, testosterone and cortisol. It is transported in the blood by lipoproteins. There are two types of lipoproteins,

1. High-Density Lipoprotein (HDL):- known as "Good Cholesterol". High levels of HDL cholesterol can lower your risk for heart disease and stroke. Adding healthy fats and omega 3 to your diet increase the HDL level.

2. Low-Density Lipoprotein (LDL):- known as "Bad Cholesterol". High levels of LDL cholesterol raise the risk for heart disease and stroke. Reduce saturated fat and trans-fat in your diet to reduce the level of LDL.

The "Vitaminia"–World of Vitamins & Minerals

A multivitamin tablet is a billion dollar industry and most used supplement in the world. Multivitamin is a combination of essential vitamins and minerals. Do we need vitamins and minerals? Yes, we need in a small amount but we do. Now the very next question, do we need multivitamin tablet? If yes, then what's the right amount? Hold on, here, take some time to think.

See, our body is the smartest machine in the world and no one can tell how many nutrients our body need every day. It only decides depending upon your lifestyle, environment and other external and internal conditions. If you are taking a balanced diet with lots of fruits and vegetables, nuts and seeds, sprouts and greens, then your body gets all the essential nutrients from the food. But if you are not having the right food, then definitely you need the help of supplements.

Antioxidants

Antioxidants are any substances which help you fight against the free radicals which are the by-product of Oxidation process. [Liver produces and uses free radicals to detoxify the body; white blood cells send free radicals to destroy bacteria, viruses and damaged cells.] When antioxidants levels in the body are lower than free radicals–due to poor nutrition, toxin exposure or other factors–bodily imbalance happened, results in many chronic diseases. Green veggies, fruits and seeds are a powerhouse of antioxidants.

Benefits of consuming antioxidants:

1. Anti-aging
2. Healthier, more youthful, glowing skin
3. Reduced Cancer risk
4. Detoxification
5. Protection against heart disease and stroke

Glycemic Index

It is a system that compares blood glucose levels and the rate of carbohydrate digestion. Simple carbohydrates are less in fiber and have a higher glycemic index. Complex carbohydates are high in fiber and have a lower glycemic index. During the time of heavy workout or athletic performances, you need foods high in glycemic index. Other than that you need carbs high in fiber and low in glycemic index.

Low GI → 0 –55 → Peas, Peanuts, Most of the fruits & vegetables, Low-fat milk & yoghurt

Moderate GI → 56 –69 → Beans, Banana, Whole wheat bread, Cheese, Popcorn, Brown rice

High GI → =70 → Rice, Bread, Potatoes, Water melon, Dates, Honey, Cornflakes

Phytonutrients

These chemicals help protect plants from germs, fungi, bugs, and other threats. When we eat phytonutrients, we get remarkable health benefits from it. They help prevent disease and keep our body working properly. Fruits and vegetables contain phytonutrients. Other plant-based foods also contain phytonutrients, such as whole grains, nuts, beans, and tea.

Different colours contain different phytonutrients,

Red Foods → Tomatoes → lycopene → Reduces the risk of cancer and heart disease

Orange Foods → Carrots → beta-carotene → Boost immune system and promotes healthy vision

Greens → Broccoli → chlorophyll → Helps control hunger

Digestive enzymes

Proteins that break down larger molecules like fats, proteins and carbs into smaller molecules that are easier to absorb across the small intestine. Without sufficient digestive enzymes, the body cannot digest food particles properly, which may lead to food intolerances. They make most of the digestive enzymes from Pineapple and papaya. We can get digestive enzymes from foods like pineapple, papaya, honey, banana and ginger.

Prebiotics & Probiotics

Your gut or digestive system is your second brain because of its activity of millions neurons to digestion process and elimination of waste through the digestive system. Inside your GI tract or digestive system, there are trillions of microbiomes like bacteria and fungi, play a major role in your metabolism, weight management, immunity and overall health. To improve your immunity and metabolism, you must increase your number of healthy gut micro biomes.

> *"The biggest influence you can have on the state of your gut lining, and a healthy microbiome is your diet–which you control."*
>
> **—J. Hyde, Author of The Gut Makeover**

(a) **Prebiotics:** Prebiotics are food for the healthy gut bacteria. Fiber or non-digestible part in the food is prebiotics, and it goes through the small intestine undigested and in the process it fermented. This fermented fiber is the best food for the healthy gut micro biomes. Add raw salads, fruits, beans, onion and garlics, whole grains to your diet to feed these healthy microorganisms.

(b) **Probiotics:** Probiotics are healthy gut bacteria that are naturally created by the process of fermentation in foods. Fermentation is a natural process that can help to make your food more digestible and improve your metabolism for the key ingredients– Gut Bacteria. Let's have a look on the fermentation process and different types of probiotics foods.

1. *Lactic acid Fermentation:* When yeasts and bacteria convert starches and sugars into lactic acid in foods like curd/yoghurt, pickles, sauerkraut, kefir, batters and breads.

2. *Ethyl alcohol Fermentation:* Here, the pyruvate molecules in starches and sugars are broken down by yeasts into alcohol and carbon dioxide molecules to produce wine and beer.

3. *Acetic acid Fermentation:* Here, fermentation of starches and sugars from grains and fruits into sour tasting vinegar like apple cider vinegar.

You don't have control over your intestinal lining, digestive systems or gut micro biomes but you can control over them through your food choices. Add prebiotics and probiotics in your diet to feed and increase the number of gut bacteria. Some foods you can add like raw fruits and vegetables, home-made pickles, low-fat yoghurt, kefir and apple cider vinegar.

Three Basic Questions

In my 2018 yoga and meditation retreat, Pondicherry, I met a celebrity coach from Australia. While discussing on health and fitness tips and tricks, he gave me this powerful techniques he used in his training to the athletes and celebrities. And it's very simple to do–just ask these three questions before eating anything.

(a) What are the ingredients in the food?

The ingredients in an apple is just the apple, ingredients in a home-made apple juice are apple, water or sugar but the ingredients in an packaged apple drink are apple juice concentrate, water, sugar, carbon dioxide, preservatives, acidity regulators, chemicals, food flavour and colours. Do you or your body need these all ingredients? From next time, while choosing your food see the ingredients. If you understand all the ingredients in the food and it contains less than five ingredients, then accept it else remove these foods from your diet to be healthy and fit.

(b) What are the nutrients in the food?

Already we discussed all the basics of nutrients in the food and now, you are well-aware of these essential nutrients. Before choosing your food, you just check the nutrients in the food and ask yourself, whether you need these nutrients to achieve your fitness goals.

(c) What is the source of the food?

This is the last question to ask before choosing your food–whether it's organic, seasonal, fresh and locally produced or not. If not then take some steps to remove the toxics out from it. The easiest way to remove toxins from food is wash them in the vinegar water.

The Hidden Nutrients–Water, Oxygen & Sunlight

The very first thing you have after coming to this beautiful world is oxygen and the last thing you will leave in this world is the same oxygen. The second thing you have is water as mother's milk and second last thing you will leave is the same water just before your last breaths. Food comes much later in your life. You can survive a month without food but can't survive a week without water and few minutes without Oxygen. That's why Water and Oxygen are macronutrients. Also, Sun is the primary source of energy as plants take it first and we animals take it from the plants. Still, you need a little amount of sunlight for hormonal balance and some essential nutrients like vitamin D. So, it considered as a micronutrient.

Water as Macronutrient

Your body composes of over 70% water and your major organs also rich in water. That's why you need a lot of water every day and it's a macronutrient. For water, just focus on these three things.

(a) **Quality of water:** To have maximum health benefits, you must drink purest form of water. Water should be clean and of higher quality. Water contamination is one of the major reasons to many diseases like diarrhoea, digestive disorder and stomach issues. To improve the quality of water, you can use a copper water bottle.

(b) **Source of water:** Our body not only get the hydration from mineral water but also from some other sources as well. Three main resources other than drinking water are fruits, vegetables and sprouts/ greens. Have them in an ample amount daily to give your body quality water for necessary hydration. You can make your water richer, by alkalizing it. The simplest way to do is get an infuser bottle and infuse the fruits and vegetables to it and keep it overnight. Drink the infused water in the very next day.

(c) **Protect from Dehydration:** In case of water, not only focus on hydration but also focus on the dehydrating agents. It's important to check on the things that dehydrates your body. Some daily intakes like tea, coffee and alcohol dehydrates your body. So, drink a little more water if you have a habit of taking these dehydrating things or limit the consumption.

Oxygen as Macronutrient

When you go to any yoga ashram or meditation retreat, the first thing they teach you is, "how to breathe well". I have attended 44 these kinds of retreats in the last 4-5 years and found this thing common in everyplace. They will teach you various breathing techniques that elevate your overall health and energy. One of my gurus once told in his speech that they used to spend many days in the Himalayas with no food and water. In those winter days, they only have air and through various breathing exercises they maintain the body temperature and energy. Most of the people use only a fraction of their lung capacity. They breathe shallowly. They become tired easily and don't know why. Through practice of deep breathing, you can concentrate the prana (life force) that increases your energy level.

Use your Diaphragm for deep breathing

The diaphragm is a muscle which divides the chest area from abdominal area. On Inhalation, the diaphragm pushes downward against the abdominal organs, gives a massage to the organs. In this process, it creates a vacuum in the lungs and air flows into them. In this way, it fills a larger part of the lungs. Exhalation occurs naturally, the diaphragm moves upward, and the abdomen moves inward, this clears the entire lung area of stagnant air. Try to do some breathing exercises like pranayama and practice deep breathing sometimes every single day or some days a week.

> *"Live in the sunshine. Swim in the sea.*
> *Drink in the wild air."*
>
> *—R. W. Emerson*

Sunlight as Micronutrient

The primary source of energy in this earth is sunlight. Most of the times, you take this energy indirectly. Plants receive this powerful energy through photosynthesis and you eat the plants. This is the first-hand energy. The other way is, plants receive the energy and animals eat them and you later, eat the animal and animal source products. This is a second-hand energy. However, sometimes you take this energy directly. If you ask anyone this simple question, why sunlight is important? The answer will be no surprise, Vitamin D. Yes, Vitamin D is a fat-soluble micronutrient, you get from sunlight. The cholesterol present under your skin forms this essential nutrient once comes contact with the sunlight.

The next big advantage of taking the sunlight directly is the sleep hormone melatonin. These sleep-friendly hormone secrets when you exposed to sunlight. To get the benefits, have some sunlight in the early morning between 6 to 9 a.m. To get the other benefits like skin improvement, boosting the immunity and getting the nutrients, you must get some sun on your skin. Just try to use your office breaks to move outside or close to the window to get this natural source of energy.

Two ways to disappear major diseases

There is only one reason for all the diseases in our life–cell malfunction. If every cells of your body, are working fine then there is no chance of diseases. And there are two main reasons for cell malfunction.

(a) **Cell Toxicity:** Poisoning our cell with all the toxins (internal & external)

(b) **Cell Deficiency:** Not providing the essential nutrients to our cells

Cell Toxicity

Toxins are the unwanted things that the body (or cells) doesn't require and have to eliminate regularly to be healthy and fit. Mainly, there are two types of toxins that make our cells toxic.

(a) **Internal Toxins:** The body creates these toxins in the digestion process and the bodily maintenance process.

(b) **External Toxins:** These toxins come from the outside environment like,

- Pesticides/chemicals used in the food industry

- Harmful minerals like lead, mercury and cadmium

- Air and Water Pollution

- Hazardous Chemicals from plastic/furniture/paint

- EMR–Electro Magnetic Radiation

- Cosmetics or beauty products like soap, shampoo, deodorant, etc

Detoxification

The process to eliminate or remove these harmful toxins from the body through different processes is known as Detoxification. There are four major organs in the body to eliminate the harmful toxins, lungs, liver, kidney and colon (large intestine). And there are four ways through which these organs eliminate toxins from the body through the detoxification process, urine, excreta, sweat and breathe.

5 Best ways to detox naturally

1. *Water-rich diet*: Our body comprises over 70% of the water. All major organs function well when water is available in the body. To remove toxins and help the toxin-removing organs, drink a lot of water and eat a water-rich diet. Add fresh fruits, vegetables, salads, juices, smoothies, sprouts and herbal teas in your diet. As a health and lifestyle coach, I recommend my clients to drink one juice every day in the morning on empty stomach–Fresh Wheat Grass Juice with no added sugar or preservatives.

2. *Physical Exercise*: The lymphatic system, is a part of your immune system, works like a drainage for your body. To provide your lymphatic system the necessary pumping and to remove toxins through sweats, do some jumping exercise. Jumping exercises are also known as anti-gravity exercises like a jumping jack, jump rope, running, stair climbing or hiking.

3. *Breathing Exercises*: Through Breathing, your body removes toxins in the form of carbon dioxide and cough. Do some breathing exercises like pranayama, deep breathing, or power breathing regularly in fresh air.

4. *Body Massage*: A 30-60 minutes of body massage removes loads of toxins from the body by improving the circulation. For a better result, take

a steam bath after the massage to remove toxins through sweating by the sweat pores. The most effective body massages are Swedish massage, Aromatherapy massage, Deep tissue massage or Thai massages.

5. *Fasting*: Fasting is an old technique of healing and toxins elimination. In the time of fasting, your body does the maintenance process and remove the unwanted waste in the form of toxins and dead cells. Do fasting like juice fasting, water fasting or even dry fasting at least once or twice a month.

Cell Deficiency

Cell deficiency happens when the cells of your body don't get the essential nutrients regularly. The essential nutrients for your cells are carbs, amino acids, essential fatty acids, vitamins, minerals, and oxygen. Apart from that they need water, sunlight, digestive enzymes and anti-oxidants to function efficiently. The best way to have all the basic nutrients is to add fresh raw nutrient-dense foods in your diet like fruits, vegetables, sprouts, greens, nuts and seeds. Some of my clients eat only an apple and banana as fruits. To get all the nutrients, you must add variety in your food plate and all the locally produced seasonal foods. Another way to reduce deficiency and adding nutrients is to have a green juice on an empty stomach first thing in the morning like wheatgrass juice or any vegetable or fruit juices.

Three Natural Body Cycle

Everything works as a cycle in this world, day and night, sun and moon, birth and death. The weather changes in the cycle, summer, rainy and winter. Similarly our body works with the nature in three natural body cycles. Our body runs through three 8-hour cycles per day.

A. *Elimination Cycle (4AM–12PM)*: Our body eliminates all the toxins and harmful chemicals in this cycle. In this cycle, you must do some exercise and sweat more. Eat water-rich diet fruit, vegetables, sprouts and greens.

B. *Welcoming Cycle (12PM–8PM)*: Our body welcomes all the major foods and nutrients in this cycle through your major meals. You must take your heavy meals in these 8 hours. Best time for the digestion process.

C. *Absorption Cycle (8PM–4AM)*: All the essential nutrients absorption occurs in this cycle. Body absorbs the nutrients and remove all the toxins to release in the elimination cycle. Eat nothing heavy in this cycle and rest well.

Dietary Supplements

When you join a gym for the first time, then, your trainers will recommend you to have a supplement. Most common recommendations are whey protein, mass gainer, multi-vitamin, CLA, Fat-burner. See, there is nothing bad to have a supplement. The only thing I recommend my clients that have your supplement but with proper understanding and with alignment of your goal and lifestyle.

"Nutritional supplements are not a substitute for a nutritionally balanced diet."

—Deepak Chopra

As the name suggest, Supplement is not a meal replacement at all. It is just an additional thing to support your overall fitness goal and lifestyle. From my research and experience, if you are having a well-balanced meal then you rarely need any supplements for just being healthy and fit. But for bodybuilders, sports people, or highly active celebrities, a supplement is a must.

There are some generic cases where you need supplements for a certain period like,

- Pregnant women need a supplement of folic acid or iron to reduce risk of birth defects

- Older people need a vitamin D to reduce the risk of osteoporosis

- Vegetarian or vegan people need a vitamin B12 supplement

- Multi-vitamins can be a part of a balanced nutrition plan

- Veg-extracted Omega-3 is a powerful supplement for all of us to protect our heart, brain and joints

Super Foods & Super Greens

Super foods are very low in calories and rich in essential nutrients. They have a very high nutritional density. Like a bowl of broccoli and a handful of pumpkin seeds can give your body many nutrients that your body cries for. You can convert your meal to a complete power-pack meal by just adding these super foods & super greens.

Super Foods

- Oats
- Broccoli
- Pumpkin & pumpkin seeds
- Almond & Walnut
- Flax seed
- Chick peas
- Spices–Turmeric, Black pepper, Cinnamon
- Ginger, Garlic
- Fruits–Pomegranate, Pineapple, Papaya & any seasonal
- Mushrooms

Super Greens

- Wheatgrass

> - Moringa
> - Dark Leafy Greens–Spinach, Kale, Lettuce & Cabbage
> - Microgreens
> - Green tea
>
> Medicinal herbs like Tulsi & Neem

5 High Pranic Food–Take it Daily

Your body is the vehicle and food is the fuel. If you have a costly vehicle, then you must use the quality extra-mile fuel not the cheaper one. Yoga and Ayurveda always believes in the food according to the energy (prana) and considered them as of higher qualities. Some yoga experts called it as sattvic diet or yogic diet. Foods you can eat include fruits, vegetables, whole grains, lentils, nuts and seeds, herbal teas, natural sugars, and healthy spices. Foods to avoid include meat and fish, fried foods, white sugar and flour, garlic, onion, spicy foods, alcohol, tobacco and stimulants. Let's make it simple. You just need to add five super pranic foods to your lifestyle. It helps to become healthy and energetic by making your blood pure and boosting your immunity.

1. *Fruits*: Fresh and colourful fruits must be part of your diet. Seasonal fruits are the gift from the nature to build immunity and enhance healing. Best time to eat fruits is on an empty stomach in the morning

hours. It helps the body to release the toxins in the elimination cycle. You can take it as juice or salads but make sure the juice and salad must be natural and fresh with no sugar and preservatives.

2. *Vegetables*: As a health and lifestyle coach, I always recommend my clients to add a rainbow of vegetables in their diet. Vegetables are the real carbohydrates as they are rich in water, full of fiber and have many vitamins and minerals. They are also a great source of plant protein, anti-oxidants and phytonutrients. Steamed and boiled vegetables are much better than roasted or fried form. To keep the digestive enzymes, you need to add fresh vegetables in your diet in juices, smoothies, and in salads.

3. *Nuts & Seeds*: Nuts and seeds are a great source of quality protein and healthy fat. It helps to increase the good cholesterol HDL and reduce the bad cholesterol LDL in your body. These are super foods for your heart, brain and joints. You can add them in your breakfast bowl, in salads or you can have a handful in your evening snack with your favourite herbal tea. Some healthy nuts include Almonds, Pistachios, Walnut, Cashew, Peanut, Pecan, and Brazil nuts. And some healthy seeds include Flax, Chia, Pumpkin, Sunflower and Sesame.

4. *Sprouts*: Sprouts are the most nutritious and local superfoods. Sprouts grows in water and it takes

2-5 days to grow. They are rich in water and many essential nutrients especially protein and digestive enzymes. Add a small bowl of sprouts daily to your salads, veggies or snacks to boost your immunity and enhancing the energy level.

5. *Micro and Leafy Greens*: Health coaches and Doctors recommend eating minimum 50-60% of raw food. Sprouts and micro greens are best raw food to add in your diet. Micro greens are little mature than sprouts and grow in the soil. Add a small bowl of micro greens and baby greens like spinach, mustard, or moringa in your lunch or dinner.

Bhagavad Gita on Food

In Chapter 17 of holy Bhagavad Gita, Shree Krishna explains Arjuna on the food and its impact on our mind and body. Lord Krishna, the master nutritionist, divides food into three categories – Sattvic, Rajsic & Tamsic.

"Whatever you do, make it an offering to me-the food you eat, the sacrifices you make, the help you give, even your sufferings."

—Bhagavad Gita

Verse–8:

आयु:सत्वबलारोग्यसुखप्रीतिविवर्धना: |
रस्या: स्निग्धा: स्थिरा हृद्या आहारा: सात्विकप्रिया: || 8||

"Persons in the mode of goodness prefer foods that promote the life span, and increase virtue, strength, health, happiness, and satisfaction. Such foods are juicy, nourishing, wholesome and naturally tasteful."

Verse–9:

कट्वम्ललवणात्युष्णतीक्ष्णरूक्षविदाहिनः |
आहारा राजसस्येष्टा दुःखशोकामयप्रदाः || 9||

"Foods that are too bitter, too sour, salty, very hot, pungent, and dry are dear to persons in the mode of passion. Such foods produce pain, misery, and disease."

Verse–10:

यातयामं गतरसं पूति पर्युषितं च यत् |
उच्छिष्टमपि चामेध्यं भोजनं तामसप्रियम् || 10||

"Foods that are overcooked, stale, putrid, polluted, and impure are dear to persons in the mode of ignorance."

Common Healthy Eating Habits

Drink your food & eat your water

Digestion always starts from the mouth as soon as you take the first bites. Your mouth always works like a grinder and Stomach works like a juicer. So, it's your duty to grind your food before sending it to the juicer to extract the nutrients. Not only the foods but also you need to chew your water or juices. In that way, it mixes well with the digestion-friendly saliva in the mouth. When you chew your food properly, you eat less and your digestion improves. It leads to weight loss and boost energy.

Emotional and Binge Eating

People eat mainly for two reason–Physical hunger and Emotional hunger. Physical hunger is the natural signal from the body when it needs energy. Food tastes better when you're hungry. Emotional hunger is just because of emotions and stress. You indulge in emotional eating when you are in an emotional state or any stressed condition. People use emotional eating as a coping mechanism to get out from the stress condition. Binge eating (eating a large amount of food quickly) happens because of our lack of focus or unawareness. Once they eat a large chunk of food, most of the binge eaters regret.

Mindful eating is the best healthy habit to avoid emotional eating or binge eating. In case of mindful eating, you completely aware of your hunger and what you are eating. Here, you may not talk, read, work, or watch TV while you are eating your food. It's a way to taste and enjoy every bite of food and also, through this practice, you can have control over the amount of food you are eating.

Stress and Food

Stress is a physical response. When you feel stressed, your body thinks it's under attack and switches to 'fight-

or-flight' mode. This 'fight-or-flight' response triggers mix of chemicals and hormones in the body like cortisol, adrenaline, and epinephrine. This causes several reactions, it shunts blood flow to your large muscles, your heart rate increases, your blood pressure goes up and it shut down unnecessary bodily functions such as digestion.

It's better to avoid eating during the time of stress. Take some deep breathe and relax before eating your food. It stimulates the parasympathetic system and hence, improves digestion. Weight gain, Obesity and Diabetes are the few diseases which happen from long-term stress.

Don't do these 5 things after having Food

There are few things to take care just after having your major meals to improve digestion and nutrient absorption. Few people think taking a nap or having a fruit is a healthy post-meal practice. Let's discuss 5 things to avoid after having food.

1. *No Smoking*: Whether it's before or after meal, smoking is harmful for the body. But smoking after a meal affects the intestines and causes a certain irritation in the gut. As per experts, smoking after a meal may increase the risk of bowel cancer.

2. *No Tea*: The acidic nature of the tea makes challenge for protein digestion. Not only that, it hampers few mineral absorption. The best time to have a tea is in the mid-morning or afternoon snacks.

3. *No Bath*: Bathing after a meal hamper digestion. During a shower, the blood in and around the stomach moves to other parts of the body, causes a delay in the digestion process. The best time to take a bath is in the morning after a quick workout in cold water.

4. *No Sleep*: Whether it after lunch or dinner, sleeping just after having food creates a conflict between your gut and brain. Acidity and Gastrointestinal disorder happened because of this. That's why it is a best practice to have your dinner early, at least 3-4 hours before your bed time.

5. *No Fruits*: Fruits are the real fast-food. It digests fast. Fruits will not be digested properly if you have them in post-meal. It can cause indigestion, acid-reflux and other digestive disorders. The best time to have fruits is on an empty stomach and in the morning.

Revise Notes

- Always remember dieting is temporary, lifestyle change is permanent.

- Focus little on the calories-count; check the nutrient-density of the foods before eating.

- Water & Oxygen are macronutrient; Sunlight is micronutrient.

- The magic formulae to make disease disappear– "Remove the Toxicity, Replace the Deficiency".

- Eat the Sattvic food and follow the common healthy eating habits.

For more on food and nutrition, check youtube.com/ alokdwibedy.

Action Exercise

1. Have you tried any diets?

2. What lifestyle changes are you planning for the next 5 weeks?

3. Write nutrient-density of some of your favourite or regular foods?

4. What are you doing for detoxification?

5. Are you drinking your food and chewing your water?

THREE

MEDITATION

"Meditation will change your life for the better, enhance your physical health, and improve your sleep, and help you achieve your goals, both material and spiritual."

—Deepak Chopra

"Training your mind to be in the present moment is the #1 key to making healthier choices."

—Susan Albers

There is one secret formula you must know–"People always notice Energy!" And to have energy in your life, you need these two things, healthy body and peaceful mind. Once you have a healthy body and a peaceful mind, you have enough energy to invest in your career/craft and relationship to achieve all the success and happiness. Just as our body needs physical exercise in order to operate with the most efficiency, so too our mind needs the mental exercise that is developed during the consistent practice of meditation. Meditation is a simple daily practice to get profound results if it is done consistently. Many famous personalities practice and spread the power of meditation are Richard Branson, Arianna Huffington, Oprah Winfrey, Deepak Chopra, and Robin Sharma. People do meditation for different reasons like holistic health, spiritual practice, increase focus and productivity, But who meditates regularly receive benefits on all these levels–physical, mental, emotional, and spiritual.

Let's mind it...

Meditation and Health

As you know, health is all about small daily choices. You take these small choices either consciously or unconsciously. In the conscious state, you mostly take the healthy choice while in an unconscious state, you take unhealthy choices. In the conscious state, you are fully aware about the importance of exercise and food in your health and you always choose healthy. Here comes the role of meditation on health as it helps you to be conscious and peaceful even in the most challenging period of your day or life. If you practice meditation regularly, it will help you in many ways.

Health Benefits of Meditation

After coming back from hospital, I was in terrible stress and felt most of the time lonely. I wasn't able to focus on my work and it affected my accuracy and productivity. Not only that, it affected my health so much I had to take anti-depressant and gained weight as well. In 2016, I went to a yoga and meditation retreat to Madurai, Tamilnadu. There I met the great Swami Hariomnandaji and learnt some easy techniques from him to practice meditation. He helped me to practice breathe mediation, walking meditation and at last, mantra meditation. He initiated me with my personal mantra and guided me to chant it daily during the meditation practice. To my surprise, within a month I felt superbly fine and for the first time in the last six month I smiled and laughed. He told me, "just keep it up, you will be good". I asked, "What swami ji! This smile?" He said, "No man, this meditation".

Few benefits from my realisation:

1. Relief from stress and anxiety by decreasing the production of stress hormone–cortisol and adrenaline.

2. Decreased blood pressure and hypertension.

3. More efficient Oxygen use by the body

4. Restful sleep; wake up like a child

5. Increases both physical and mental energy

Meditation and Weight Loss

Traditional weight loss programs mostly focus on exercise and diet. They don't work on the most important part–our mind. Because of this, most of these programs are not sustainable. It works like a quick-fix formula and fails in the long-run process. Some people ask me, how sitting meditation burn calories and help us in weight loss. They are not aware that our body is just a vehicle with a powerful driver called mind. Our mind controls our body, and our thoughts become our reality. So, if you meditate and visualise in mind on losing weight, you can control your thoughts, emotions and feelings. And because of this simple practice, you will do regular exercise and avoid emotional eating.

People eat for two reasons, Physical hunger and Emotional hunger.

1. **Physical Hunger:** It is the natural signal from the body when it needs foods or energy. Food tastes better when you're hungry. Through regular meditation practice, with awareness, you only eat the right amount of food your body needs.

2. **Emotional Hunger:** People generally indulge in emotional eating when they feel stressed. Emotional eating used as a coping mechanism to get out from the stress condition (sometimes sex can help). Meditation and deep breathing can help you to become calm and stress-free without indulging in emotional eating. Another eating habit that leads to weight gain is Binge eating (eating a large amount of food quickly). It mainly happens because of lack of presence and awareness. Mediation can help you to avoid these binge eating situations.

Meditation and Happy Hormones

Happy hormones are those that make you happy and feel good. Some happy hormones are dopamine, endorphins, serotonin and oxytocin. Lack of these powerful hormones leads to stress, loneliness, depression, anxiety, food cravings and sleeping disorder. Then you need anti-depressants like sertraline (Zoloft), citalopram (Celexa), and fluoxetine (Prozac). But the question is, how could you boost these happy hormones without the help of any drugs?

There are many ways you can do it naturally, physical activity, proper diet, meditation and exposure to sunlight. Meditation especially mindfulness and gratefulness, is the easier ways to boost these powerful chemicals. Studies from Yale and Washington University have shown that mindfulness meditation increases your brain's levels of neurotransmitters including GABA, DHEA, melatonin, serotonin and endorphins.

Serotonin: The scientific name is the 5-HT and mainly found in the brain, gut and blood platelets. It is responsible for maintaining mood balance and absence of this leads to depression and cravings. Mindfulness aims to help an individual to be more aware of thoughts and feelings rather than reacting to them. It's an effective way to get serotonin boosts in your brain naturally.

DHEA: It stands for Dehydroepiandrosterone. It's an adrenal steroid hormone made by the adrenal gland and is then converted into androgens, oestrogens, and other hormones. These are hormones that regulate fat and mineral metabolism, sexual and reproductive function, and energy levels. Absence of these hormone leads to aging skin, erectile dysfunction, and osteoporosis. DHEA level gradually start to decline with ages, leads to many diseases and accelerate aging. Meditation provides a dramatic boost in DHEA level. Researchers discovered that meditation practioners have an incredible 43.77% more DHEA over non-practioners.

So, in short, is Meditation the fountain of Youth? Many scientists say, YES.

Meditation and Stress

"Meditation is the antidote to all the poison of your life."

Stress is a physical response. When we were a hunter gatherer, this stress helped us to protect us from the lion. When we feel stressed, our body thinks it is under attack and switches to "fight or flight" mode. Either we fight with the lion or flight/run away from the lion. But in this modern lifestyle, we feel stress most of the times and neither we do any physical work/fight nor we do any kind of movement/flight. That's why health and lifestyle coaches mentioned, "Stress is a silence killer".

The "fight or flight" response triggers mix of chemicals and hormones in the body like cortisol, adrenaline, and epinephrine. This causes a chain of reactions, blood flow is shunted to your large muscles, your heart rate increases, your blood pressure goes up and it shuts down unnecessary bodily functions such as digestion. Our body has a beautiful self-repair mechanism that fights cancer, prevent infection, and protect us from foreign bodies. However these self-repair mechanisms get deactivated when our body is full of stress hormones and in "fight-or-flight mode". My health coach once said, "The only place to take stress is your gym or health club".

Meditation helps to reverse the effects of stress response. Through a regular meditation practice, your mind become calm and silence. Meditation reduces stress hormone like cortisol and adrenaline. It also increases the happy hormones like dopamine, serotonin, and endorphins. Researchers found that just weeks after a practice of meditation, mental and physical stress relieved dramatically. As Sadhguru said, "Meditation is the only way to freedom from stress as it is a dimension beyond the mind. All the stress and struggle are of the mind."

Machine without Manual—MIND

Mind is the greatest tool of the world which works 24*7. This smartest machine creates all the machines of the world starting from your shoes to your latest smartphone. And all the tools and machines come with a how-to-use user manual. But what about the mind, Do you have a manual for it? No, the smartest machine of the world doesn't have a manual. The next question is, can you make a manual for the mind? Yes, but you can make only your own manual. You can't make a manual for other people as they are completely different from you. Their finger print, retina scan and DNA are different from you so as mind. That's why they say, "You can't hire someone to do meditation for you". And the very first step towards making your own mind manual is to understand how it works. When you go to any monastery or meditation centre or Yoga ashram, the first thing they will teach you, "How our mind works" through different meditation.

"The mind is everything. What you think you become."

—Buddha

Mind is like a Monkey

Mind is very restless and jumpy like a monkey, jumping from one tree to another. And it is constantly chattering. Mind is jumping from past events to the present and again to the future plan. It is constantly replaying the past events and planning for the future. This monkey mind is giving you opinion every time. Through breathe meditation you can control this constant jumping and chattering of this monkey mind. Simply be aware of your breath and practice, "Breathe IN, Breathe OUT".

Mind is like a Horse

Mind is like an untamed wild horse. It doesn't like to be tamed and wants to go its own way. But through regular practice and patience, you can have control over this mind. Remember, "Mind is a terrible master and a wonderful servant". So, be gentle with the mind as well be strong too and make it a wonderful servant.

Mind is like a Lake

Mind is like a lake and every thought is like a wave. The mind constantly has thought waves. A clear lake has no waves (pure mind), a wavy lake has few waves (confused mind) and a muddy lake has so many waves and distorts (disturbed mind). To have a pure and calm mind, you need to just settle down and just let it be. Here is an interesting story of Buddha.

Once, Buddha was walking from one town to another with a few of his disciples. While they were passing a lake, Buddha told one of his disciples, "I am thirsty. Do get me some water from the lake."

The disciple gladly obliged and walked up to the lake. At that moment, a bullock cart started crossing through the lake. As a result, the water became very muddy and turbid. The disciple thought, "How can I give this muddy water to Buddha to drink?"

So he came back and told Buddha, "The water in there is very muddy. I don't think it is fit to drink."

After hour later, again Buddha asked the same disciple to go back to the lake.

The disciple went back and found that the water was still muddy. He returned and informed Buddha about the same.

After sometime, again Buddha asked the same disciple to go back.

This time, the disciple found the mud had settled down, and the water was clean and clear. So he collected some water in a pot and brought it to Buddha.

Buddha looked at the water, and then he looked up at the disciple and said," See what you did to make the water clean. You let it be, and the mud settled down on its own

— and you got clear water. Your mind is exactly like that. When it is disturbed, just let it be. Give it some time. It will settle down on its own. You don't have to put any effort to calm your mind. It will happen. It's effortless."

Mind and Awareness

The smallest unit of the mind is thoughts. The mind creates thoughts. Thoughts come and go but the awareness or consciousness is constant. There is a difference between your awareness and mind. You are pure awareness but you are not your mind. Through meditation, you can control over your awareness and passing thoughts.

Meditation and Types

Meditation is a technique to observe the thoughts in the mind and let it go without any attachment. As a beginner, you can start practicing sitting meditation for some minutes but later you can meditate in every action. Through meditation you can make your thought waves (vrittis) calm and mind peaceful. The most important thing you need to meditate is concentration.

Concentration and Meditation

Concentration is the ability to do one thing at a time, instead of jumping from one subject to another. It is just focusing on one thought and giving undivided attention to just one thing. If you focus the rays of the sun through a lens, they can burn cotton or piece of paper, but the scattered rays can't do this act. Concentration is focusing the mind on one single thought. Practicing asana and pranayama will steady the mind, remove tossing and increase the power of concentration. Whatever work you do, do with perfect concentration. Never leave the work without finishing it completely. The best exercise to practice concentration is, observing the second hand of your watch for some minutes or listens to someone mindfully for few hours a day. I practiced the listening exercise with my wife and manager. It improved both my personal and professional relationship.

Once you become good with concentration, you apply the power of concentration on your meditation practice. In Raja Yoga, concentration comes before meditation. The eight limbs of Raja Yoga are Yama, Niyama, Asana, Pranayama, Pratyahara, Dhyana (Concentration), Dharana (Meditation) and Samadhi. Meditation is observing the thoughts and Concentration is for how many minutes/hours you can observe. In a term of the process, Concentration can lead to meditation.

Multitasking is a Myth

Mind can think and focus on one thought or object at a time. When we do several things at the same time, we are actually moving our attention quickly from one thing to another; it only seems to us that we are focusing on several tasks at the same time. With Multitasking, we split our attention and move our focus from one thing to another, and hence, lose energy and time, and might do mistakes and errors.

Breathe Meditation

This is a simplest way to practice meditation anytime and anywhere. As your breath is always with you, you can do it at your home or workplace or even inside your car. Here, you need to observe your breath and synchronise it with a count. Sit quietly and a count of four, inhale and with a count of four, exhale. While inhaling, feel the positive healing energy coming inside of you and at the time of exhaling, feel like releasing all the tension and worries. A five minute of quick breathe meditation can make your mind calm and peaceful.

Walking Meditation

I learnt this wonderful mediation practice in my yoga vacation to Madurai. This simple practice not only makes your mind calm but also increases your overall energy level. Like the breathe meditation, synchronise your breath with the count of your steps. Inhale, and move four steps forward and Exhale, move another four step forward. Adjust your steps as per your breathing capacity. While walking, make sure to practice silence and be mindful of your each step while touching the ground. The ancient Yogis hiked many mountains using this meditation technique.

Guided meditation

In this meditation, teacher or guide lead you through processes using all your senses either in person or via an audio, video or verbal recording. It can be a short session or as long as several hours. There are many free sources available to practice or you can use some apps like Headspace, Calm, etc. If possible join a local meditation class or hire a trainer to practice with him. The trainer will guide with your meditation practice as well help you to clear your doubts and queries.

Mantra Meditation

In this meditation practice, you need to repeat a word or sound to focus the mind and get the calmness. Sit in a relax position in a quiet place and take some deep breaths to flow oxygen to the brain. It will help to settle the mind before you start your mantra chanting. Now start chanting or reciting your personal mantra if you have any or just chant the universal mantra "OM". Few mantras to use in your practice is, "Om NamahSivaya", "Om NamoNarayana", "Om Sri MahaLakshmiNamah", "OM", "SOHAM" etc. It's better to have your personal mantra through mantra initiation. In this case, you choose your own mantra as per your ista-devata. I got my personal mantra in a temple from my Yoga teacher in my Yoga retreat.

Guide to Meditation

"Conquer your mind and conquer the world."

—*Guru Nanak*

There are certain rules to practice meditation. It's important to know the tools and techniques of meditation before practicing it. Sitting meditation is best for the beginners. Few things to be aware for sitting meditation are the time, place, sitting posture and point of concentration.

Posture and Position

The best sitting position for meditation is a firm and steady posture with spine and neck erect. Make sure to be comfortable without any pain in the joints. A comfortable cross-legged posture provides a firm base for the body and flow of energy. You can place your hands on the top of your knees in some mudras or over your lap. The best sitting position is the traditional full-lotus or half-lotus. However, if you are not able to sit in lotus pose, you can choose any comfortable position to start the practice but make sure to have an erect spine. The practice of yoga asana will strengthen your back, making it easy to sit comfortably.

Time and Place

It's best to have a neat and clean portion of your room for meditation. Don't use this place for other time of your day and make it free from any distractions. Place some altars to make it a sacred place. You can use some organic incense sticks before practicing. The best time to practice is brahmamuhurta(between 3 to 6 am). However you can practice at any time of the day especially in dawn and dusk. Regularity of time, place and practice gives a boost to your practice. If you practice in the same place every day then a flow of positive energy will be there. And if you practice in the same time, then it works like a reminder of your mind to practice. Remember, Consistency with the practice is the key.

Point of concentration

For intellectual people, the point of focus should be the space between the eyebrows (Agyanchakra) and for emotional people; it should be the heart plexus (Anahatachakra). If you are not sure whether you are more intellectual or more emotional, just go for a comfortable point. The point of concentration will help you at the time of visualisation. If you are doing meditation with open eyes, then choose some external points like a picture of your ishta-devat or a point on the wall.

Mind as a movie screen

In the movie screen, the pictures come and go but it can't affect the screen. The screen is just a reflector for all the pictures. Our mind exactly works like a screen in a meditative state, thoughts come and go but it can't disturb the awareness and mind. While practicing the meditation, just try to observe the thought waves and don't attach to them.

Asana & Pranayama for meditation

A healthy body and peaceful mind are inseparable. They form a strong base for a wonderful life. Concentration and meditation is not possible if you have pain in your body. See, now you are reading this book and you forgot that you have a head. But when you have a headache, then you suddenly feel that you have a head. Likewise, if you have pain in your body parts, then it is difficult to bring focus to your point of concentration. That's why in Raja Yoga, Asana and pranayama comes much before concentration and meditation. Through regular practice of asana and pranayama, you will have a perfect pain-free body to practice the meditation in a certain posture. Practice the asana that makes your spine erect and joint relaxes like Paschimothanasana, Bhujangasana, Dhanurasana, Ardha-matsyendrasana, and Pada-hasthasana. Practice pranayama and deep breathing to increase the energy like kapalbhati, anuloma-viloma, abdominal or yogic breathing and power breathing.

Mindfulness–Master of all meditation

Sitting meditation is the beginner's practice. Once you practice the sitting meditations and have some level of control over your mind, then you can move to the master of all meditations–Mindfulness Meditation. In this meditation, you will learn to meditate in every action. This type of meditation helps in pain relief and useful for those suffering from anxiety and depression. Few mindfulness practices are mindful breathing, mindful eating, mindful walking and body scan meditation.

> *"If you are depressed, you are living in the past.*
> *If you are anxious you are living in the future.*
> *If you are at peace, you are living in the present."*
>
> **—Lao Tzu**

Slow down your all action

The first step towards the mindfulness practice is slowing down all your day-to-day activities. You are always in the so-called busy mode and running from one place to other. Here, you need to stop for some time and calm your mind. By slowing down your actions, you will enjoy the process rather worrying about the task completion. Now, think about your bath today/yesterday, did you enjoy that? What about the last meal you had? See, this process simply tells us that happiness is just a journey not a destination. Enjoy every bit of this beautiful journey called life.

24*7 Meditations

As the name suggests, you can practice this meditation in each and every actions of your day. Starting from your morning activities to your job/career or even in your other activities, you can practice this meditation.

Just be mindful with each action you do. Mindful eating will help you to choose the right nutrients and leads to weight management and well nourishment. Mindful walking releases the stress level and enhances the energy. Add mindfulness to your regular activities like brushing your teeth and bathing. You can add some good habits like while brushing your teeth, just recite that today you will chew your food properly and use your word carefully. Similarly, while taking the bath, feel the gratefulness for getting the water from river to your bathroom and think that you are washing all the negative energy and pain out from your body.

We lose more energy in lack of mindfulness like accidents

If you are mindful with your activities, you can avoid many accidents in your life. Due to lack of mindfulness, many road accidents happen and not only that, many small accidents like falling down in the bathroom to cutting fingers in the kitchen. As a health and lifestyle coach, I found my clients are very much careful about their workout and diet but due to lack of mindfulness, they get admitted to the hospital for months due to some silly accidents. Practice mindfulness and save your health and energy.

Choose your own Model for Practice

After practicing 3-4 years of several meditations in different ashrams and retreats and through online courses, what I found is the best way to practice meditation is designing your own meditation. The best part of designing your own meditation is, it will be interesting and enjoyable. I designed this 5 step meditation in 2018 and practicing regularly.

Step 1: *Forgiveness & Gratefulness*

I start my meditation practice with these key practices. First, I forgive everyone to be feeling lighter and find few things to be grateful in my life. I just recite like, I am complete & enough.

Step 2: *Breathe Meditation*

Then, I take a few deep breaths and later, synchronise my breath with some counts. Generally, Inhale with a count of 4, hold with a count of 4 and exhale with a count of 4. After few breathe, I feel calm and peaceful. Then I moved to the next steps.

Step 3: *Observant*

I observe the thought waves in my mind and watch them carefully. See, observant is always powerful. Imagine, sometimes you give advice to the best cricketers or soccer players on TV and it's right as you are the observant. You have the power to observe the event carefully.

Step 4: *Visualisation*

This is the time to revise the purpose statement and goals of my life. I visualise the ideal day and life in these 2-3 minutes of practice.

Step 5: *Feel the Oneness & protecting source*

This is the final step of my 5-step meditation. Here, I practice the advaita principle i.e., no-duality. All are same and comes from the same source. It makes my meditation more powerful.

Revise Notes

- Exercise gives us health of the body. Meditation gives us health of the mind.

- There are many health benefits of meditation like weight loss, hormonal balance, reducing stress and anxiety.

- Remember, Mind is the smartest machine in the world comes with no manual. You have to make your own manual.

- Choose the right type of meditation for you and start practicing daily. Mindfulness is the master meditation.

To know more about meditation, visit:
youtube.com/alokdwibedy

Action Exercise

1. Write down the place and time of the meditation practice.

2. Have you ever experienced magic of meditation?

3. Do you have a personal mantra?

4. Which meditation you are going to practice from today?

5. Write few ways to practice concentration in day-to-day life.

RELAXATION

"Sometimes, the most productive thing you can do is relax."

—Mark Black

"Health requires this relaxation, this aimless life. This life in the present,"

—Henry David Thoreau

Our body and mind works like all other machines of the world. All machines in the world need a little resting period for cooling down and increasing efficiency. We are very much aware of this but forget to give a resting period to our body and mind. Many have been forgotten that rest and relaxation are nature's way of recharging. In this so-called modern being-busy world, we are living a super-busy go-go-go lifestyle. We wake up stressed, get ready for our daily job without giving a pause, spend a wholeday in our being-busy-less-productive job, come back home with lack of energy, spend the rest time to watch TV or Netflix and then retire to a restless sleep. A few years ago, it was not the case. We had a lot of time to rest and relax with ourself, family and community. But in this modern, social-media friendly world, we are living a box-lifestyle. We are spending most of our time inside the concrete-boxes (home, office, malls) and in front of the digital boxes (laptop, cell phone, TV). Ask yourself, when you spent your last quality me-time without your electronic devices? In our so-called busy life, it is very difficult to relax. Also, when the body and mind are constantly overworked, their natural efficiency diminishes. To be healthy, we focus more on exercise and nutrition but forget this important pillar of lifestyle. It helps us to increase the productivity, improve the quality of sleep, reduce the stress level and avoid many small accidents. A quick power-breathing session or a relaxing15 minutes break from your work or just read a book over a cup of herbal tea works like wonder. That's why people who are supremely creative like Darwin, Einstein, or da-Vinci rested in between their creative projects. Research found that, most successful students napped more and slept longer.

Let's relax...

What is Relaxation?

Once I got to know that I am in depression and taking anti-depressants from my sister-in-law (she's a doctor and checked my medicines), I checked with my doctor to stop the medication. And the very next day, set up a one-on-one meeting with my manager to discuss my unplanned vacation. I booked a resort in Matheran (Asia's no.1 pollution free city) and spent four days there without my cell-phone. After this quick mini-vacation, I went to Pondicherry for a yoga and meditation retreat and enjoyed one week of complete relax and spiritual life. These ten days relaxation retreat in Matheran and Pondicherry helped me to bounce back from my exhausted and depressed life. I became more peaceful and productive in my life and career.

What I learnt from my first experience and from the four years of research is rest and relaxation help you do better and enjoy life more. Relaxation is not the same as laziness. Watching TV for hours being a couch-potato is not the right way to relax in your life. Even while trying to rest and relax, you are wasting lots of mental and physical energy through tension. Relaxation is when the body and mind are free from tension and anxiety. A proper relaxation rejuvenates your body and mind.

Types of Relaxation

I learnt the techniques of relaxation through my Yoga practices. As a Yoga trainer, I often give importance to relaxation in my sessions. Yoga prescribes a period of complete relaxation, when practically no energy or 'prana' being consumed. That's why my Guru said, "one hour of Yoga practice is equal to one hour of exercise, one hour of deep breathing and one hour of relaxation".

1. *Physical Relaxation:* Our organs and movements work from the instructions of mind through thoughts. Thoughts from the mind convert into the required action. In case of physical relaxation, you can instruct the mind to relax the organs and muscles. This process is called autosuggestion and the relaxation position is known as Savasana. After practicing some deep breathing and asana sequence, you can lie down in savasana and instruct your mind to relax each body parts and internal organs. This process is also known as "Body-scan Meditation".

2. *Mental Relaxation:* Even if you are physically relaxed, still some energy leaks through random thoughts and unnecessary worries. In case of mental relaxation, besides physical relaxation, you

are focusing on your breath. Once you synchronise your breath with certain counts, you will become calm and peaceful. There is no place of stress and anxiety in your mind.

3. *Complete Relaxation:* This is called "Yogic relaxation or Spiritual relaxation". This is the advance version of mental relaxation. Through mental relaxation, one can't completely calm or relax the mind. Throughout the day, you are facing many challenging situations with evil emotions like anger, jealous, fear, sorrows, stress, and anxiety. To deal with such a situation, you need to think yourself beyond the physical body and mind. You are a pure soul and self. This identification with the self, gives the complete relaxation. Remember, "You are Enough".

Breathing Technique

Breathing is the most simple and quick way to give relaxation to the body and mind. Even in the most stressful situation in your life and job, with some deep or power breathes, you can feel relax and calm. Most people breathe shallowly and become tired.When you go any yoga vacation or retreat, the first thing they teach you is the "power of breathing". Through breathing practices, you can have control over the thoughts. Control of the thoughts leads to control the mind.

"Breathing in, there is only the present moment.
Breathing out, it is a wonderful moment."

—Thich Nhat Hanh

Deep Breathing

Deep breathing is one of the best ways to release stress from the body and mind. When you breathe in, your body receives oxygen and releases carbon dioxide. Shallow or improper breathing leads to less oxygen flow to blood cells results into fatigue, stress and anxiety. When you breathe deeply, cells get maximum energy through the oxygen in the blood and lungs removes lots of toxins through breathe out. The only requirement for practicing deep breathing is fresh air. Research found that six deep breaths are enough to give instant relaxation from any stressful situation.

Power Breathing

Stress comes to your life when you have low energy. Power breathing is a technique to increase your energy and enhancing the healing power. A major amount of toxins from the body are removed through the lungs. A minimum of ten power breathes 2-3 times daily is enough to eliminate toxins and give you proper relaxation by releasing the stress. It is very simple to do and take only a few minutes. Sit with back straight on the ground or on a chair and relax your body. Inhale for 3/4/5 seconds as per your capacity and then hold for 12/16/20 seconds. And then slowly exhale in 6/8/10 seconds. See, the ratio must be Inhale:Hold:Exhale = 1:4:2.

Diaphragm Breathing

Shallow breathing is the number one cause for fatigue and tiredness in day-to-day life. That's why breathe training is a must for most of the competitive athletes to increase the endurance and overall energy. Diaphragm breathing is a deep breathing practice using the diaphragm muscles. Diaphragm is a muscle that divides the chest area from abdominal area. On Inhalation, the diaphragm pushes downward against the abdominal organs that gives a massage to the organs and creates a vacuum in the lungs and air flows into them. This way, it fills largest part of the lungs. Exhalation occurs naturally, the diaphragm moves upward, and the abdomen moves inward, this clears the entire lung area of stagnant air. It's very easy to practice. Just sit straight or lie down and keep your one hand over the belly. Inhale deeply so that the hand pushes forward maximum and exhale to move the hand inward. Make sure to have fresh air while practicing and practice for 5-10 minutes daily.

Wim Hoff Breathing Technique

"The breath knows how to go deeper than the mind."

—Wim Hoff

This is special breathing technique given by the superman Wim Hoff. He is the Iceman and has Guinness world records for swimming under ice. He claims, with this simple breathing practice and cold explosion,you can activate your parasympathetic nervous system that boost your immunity and help you calm and relax. Sit in a comfortable position in a quiet place and take 30-50 quick, deep breaths, inhaling through nose and exhaling through mouth. Then, take a deep breath and exhale completely; hold until you need to breathe in. Inhale again fully and hold it for 10-20 seconds. This is one round of Wim Hoff breathing. Repeat at least 2-3 times to get the maximum benefits. If you want to take the cold shower, then you can practice in the bathroom while standing. Be a little careful and listen to your body while practicing.

Air-filtering plants

For complete relaxation, a healthy home environment is mandatory. Besides a positive environment, fresh air is a must and houseplants contribute to it in many ways.They are the cheapest and best air-purifiers. There are many harmful toxins and pollutants like Benzene, Ammonia, formaldehyde, and xylene in the air especially in the cities. Also, incense sticks used in the prayer have more chemicals and as dangerous as cigarettes. These pollutants and chemicals have adverse effects on our overall health and leads to diseases like lungs infection, headache, and irritation in the eye. As per NASA clear air study, there are few indoor plants helps in removing these hazardous chemicals and pollutants.

1. Spider Plant

2. Snake Plant (Mother-in-law's tongue)–Best for the bedroom

3. Erica Palm–Best for the living room

4. Money Plant

5. Aloe Vera

All about Sleep and Sex

Hormones are like messengers in the body and responsible for different bodily functions. The three things that help hormonal balance in the body are Sleep, Sunlight & Sex. That's why health coaches mentioned them as "Power of 3S". Melatonin, Growth hormone, Dopamine and Oxytocin are some important healthy and happy hormones secreted because of these 3S.

Importance of Sleep

You can live four days without water, about twenty-five days without food and about six days without sleep. Then, what's more important; Sleep or Food? It's very simple to answer, sleep. We are always focusing on exercise and diet. We are missing the third element of the stool–Sleep. Sleep is the #1 missing elements to living a leaner, looking younger and feeling sexier. As one of the fittest actors in Bollywood John Abraham said in an interview, "The three most important pillars of his fitness regime are, Diet, Exercise and Rest/Recovery i.e. Sleep."

Quality vs. Quantity

When it comes to sleep, it's always considered as quality vs. quantity. A few hours of quality deep sleep is more valuable than many hours of restless sleep. The most important parameter to check the sleep quality is your sleep schedule and the feeling after you wake up. Doctors and health experts recommend 7-8 hours of sleep every day but it depends on your lifestyle and the environment. Sleep is a basic need but if you live a stress-free life with full awareness and on a clean diet, you can reduce your sleep gradually without affecting your health and energy. A few hours of quality sleep gives your body the best possible relaxation.

"Sleep is the best meditation."

—Dalai Lama

10 Best tips to have high Quality Sleep

A quality sleep rebuilds you and keeps you young and energetic. High quality sleep boosts your immunity, balances your hormone, improve your metabolism, and enhance both physical and mental energy. And Sleep deprivation leads to digestion issues, increase your appetite, trigger the stress-hormone and poor food choices. Here, the top 10 tools and techniques to hack your sleep tonight,

1. Get 15-30 minute of sunlight in the morning to balance the hormone–Melatonin.

2. Fix your best sleep schedule and try to stick to it. Go to bed at the right time and wake up at the same time every day.

3. Do some physical activity regularly. Avoid heavy workout at least 3 hours before bed time.

4. Reduce your caffeine intake. Stop taking caffeine or caffeinated beverages post 5 pm.

5. Say No to the screens at least 1- 2 hours before bedtime. No mobile, TV, laptop, or any blue light.

6. Get an afternoon nap or weekend extra-sleep to adjust the sleep-debt over the week.

7. Practice little deep breathing and meditation to calm the thought waves before sleep.

8. Check your Diet. Add Magnesium-rich food like pumpkin seeds and Brazil nuts to enhance the sleep quality.

9. Arrange your bedroom to a perfect place for relax and sleep. Check the temperature and add some air-filtering plants in the bedroom.

10. Read a paperback book just before to sleep especially a cool novel, biography or self-development books.

Sex and Stress

Sex, stress and sleep are linked in many ways.A good sex can release the stress you get after a stressful day or week. A strong physical affection and healthy sexual behaviour with a partner lowers the stress level and enhances the mood. Health experts considered sex as best stress management components. A sense of touch through massages and warm hugs, secrets one of the happy-hormones Oxytocin and it is a great stress reliever. The other feel-good hormone releases through sexual activity is endorphin. This hormone helps your body and mind relax and give you an instant positive mood.

Tips for better satisfying Sex

In case of sex relaxation and satisfaction, it's not all about more sex but better sex. A better sex after a stressful day gives you much needed relaxation. Few lifestyle tips to improve your sexual intimacy are,

1. Make your relationship healthy with proper understanding. This is the first steps towards a satisfying sex.

2. Improve your communication. Use your words mindfully and listen carefully.

3. Get enough sleep to improve your growth and sex hormones.

4. Eat healthy fat like nuts and seeds especially pumpkin seeds to increase the good cholesterol. To produce the sex hormones like testosterone, your body requires a good amount of fat and cholesterol.

5. Do some physical activity regularly like strength training. It helps to improve your stamina and the larger muscles contribute to higher testosterone.

Fasting 101

What we do when we feel sick or attacked by a virus or flu. We go to a doctor, Yes or No? Now think what animals do in the jungle when they feel the same. Do they have a doctor? How they recover from the disease and discomfort? No, they don't have a doctor. They use their internal healing mechanism. They take help from the nature and its healing power. And the nature's best way of recovering/healing is Fasting.

The first thing they do is, stop eating and give a rest to the digestive system. And then they find a comfortable place with fresh air and sunlight to have complete rest and relax. Like the cows stop eating and the dogs and cats, eat grass to vomit and give complete rest to the gut and body. Fasting is one of the best ways to give relaxation to the body and increase the healing power. The best time to do fasting is at the time of seasonal change to avoid common diseases.

Difference between Fasting and Starvation

Fasting is a technique to improve will-power and boost the overall immunity or healing power through proper relaxation. Starvation is suffering caused by lack of food.

Biology of Fasting

When you fast, your brain takes it as a challenge and takes the necessary actions. First, for a few hours (12-18hours) without food, your body uses the stored glycogen in liver. After using the glycogen, it then moves to the Fat, the stored form of energy. The process of using fats for energy is called *ketosis*. It helps in weight management. The energy used for food digestion (TEF) now used to removing the toxins and dead cells from the body and repairing of the cells and tissues.

"The best of all medicines are resting and fasting."

—Benjamin Franklin

Benefits of Fasting

Fasting is a natural healer. And it is the best form of relaxation for the body and mind. There are many benefits of fasting starting from detox to resting and healing.

1. It is the best technique to practice self-discipline and control the mind. It increases the will-power.

2. It helps to burn the extra calories in the form of stored glycogen and fat that leads to weight management.

3. It detoxifies the blood and all major organs. And it helps to remove toxins from various organs like colon, liver, kidneys, lungs, and skin.

4. It makes the mind calm and relaxes with the pure and clear thoughts.

5. You can cure many diseases through right form of fasting. Animals use this powerful technique to heal their body.

6. Fasting stimulates the growth hormone, that is responsible for increase the muscle mass, better protein-synthesis, and strengthening the bones by retaining the calcium.

7. Regular fasting reverses many lifestyle diseases like cancer, diabetes, blood pressure, skin diseases and Alzheimer's diseases.

8. Fasting is also good for your heart as after 12-14 hours of fasting,body started using LDL cholesterol or the bad cholesterol.

Types of Fasting

Fasting can be of different types depending upon the food and duration. Some popular fasting with many health benefits are,

1. *Fruit Fasting*: It is a very popular form of fasting and it is good for beginners and one-day fasts. You can do 1-day, 3-day or even 7-day fruit fasting. A very common question I faced, is sugar in fruits affect the fasting? No, the sugar in fruit is Fructose. Unlike glucose, it has a slow break down process. There are two ways to do fruit fasting. The one-fruit fast, is a mono-diet where you can eat only one fruit throughout the fasting period and any fruit fast, which allows to take any fruits except the fleshy fruits like banana.

2. *Juice Fasting*: It is a fad diet in which a person consumes only fruit and vegetable juices. It is very helpful in detoxification and weight loss. You can't do this fasting for longer periods. If want to do, then can do with proper medical guidance or with an expert guidance. The only thing to care here is to avoid fleshy food like banana.

3. *Water Fasting*: In this fasting, no foods or juices allowed to eat or drink. The only thing allowed here is water. It can be mineral water or alkalize water. Drink water on a regular interval. If want to do for a longer period, then medical advice required. Don't do any vigorous exercise during water fasting.

4. *Dry Fasting*: Dry fasting restricts the liquid and food both. You can't even have water in this fasting period. The health experts recommend doing dry fasting at least once or twice a month increases overall health benefits. One day of dry fasting is said to be equivalent to three days of water fasting. During the dry fasting, on absence of water from outside, your body makes its own water. It breaks the stored fat to get the hydrogen and get Oxygen from the breathing to prepare the water (H2O). It is the most pure form of water and helps to detox the body.

5. *Intermittent Fasting*: In IF, it is not required to eat less but to only reduce the window of eating. This is

also known as Window fasting. There are different ways to do it.

(a) *5:2 Ratio:* Here, you can eat normally for 5 days in a week and then reduce the calorie intake to 500 Cal (1/4th of the total calorie) in other two days.

(b) *16:8 Ratio:* You can do this fasting regularly and add it to your lifestyle. You can eat only during 8 hours window a day. For next 16 hours, you have to go for fasting. You can choose your windows as per your current lifestyle. Suppose you have your dinner at 6 pm and break your fast with the breakfast in the next morning at 10 am. It's a 16:8 intermittent fasting. In the fasting window, you can have water or even herbal teas.

Journaling

Journaling is a great stress-management tool. It improves your emotional strength through self-analysis. While writing in your journal, you get a most reliable friend to share your thoughts and feelings on any stressful event and situation in your life. And the most important thing is, it's personal. The great Bruce Lee used this technique to manage his stress level. He writes all the negative thoughts and events in a paper and then burnt it to remove it from the mind. Journaling is a great way to remove the bad thoughts from your mind through your hand to the papers.

"Journal writing is a wonderful pathway to self-awareness."

—Rand Olson

The Can't Control list

Someone well said, "You can control only three things in your life, the thoughts you think, the words you speak and the actions you do." There are many things you can't control in life.

But you get stressed for these silly and frivolous things in your day-to-day life. For example, the other people's opinion or behaviour or the weather changes or a delay in your flight or travel schedule. By making a "Can't control" list in your journal and understanding them, you can just let them go and relax. Instead of feeling stressful to this situation, you can accept as it is and use the phrase, "Everything is right". Few things from my journal are,

(1) The weather (2) Traffic (3) The Past events (4) Other people's Opinion (5) Any Changes.

I wrote few stories in my journal on this topic and this is my favourite story.

There is an old story of a farmer and his horse. One day his horse ran away. Upon hearing the news, his neighbours came to visit. "We're so sorry about your horse. Such bad luck!" they said sympathetically.

"Maybe, who knows" the farmer replied.

The next morning the horse returned, bringing with it 12 other wild horses from the jungle. "How wonderful, you must be lucky" the neighbours exclaimed.

"Maybe, who knows" replied the farmer.

The following day, his son tried to ride one of the untamed horses, was thrown, and broke his leg. The neighbours again came to offer their sympathy for what they called his "misfortune."

"Maybe, who knows" said the farmer.

The very next day, military officials came to the village to draft strong and fit young men into the army. Seeing that the son's leg was broken, they spared him by. The neighbours came back again to congratulate the farmer on his great fortune.

"Maybe, who knows" answered the farmer with a smile.

Goal and Purpose statement

A journey without a destination is stressful and confusing. You need a specific goal or purpose too in the life's journey to make it a wonderful and memorable one. Life is all about marathon not a 100m sprint. So, in your journal, write the purpose for living and set some achievable goals for the next decades. Build a dream bucket list and just go for it.

Forgiveness and Gratefulness Page

You need to be very much careful of your desires. Desires if fulfilled then convert into greed else anger. Anger is one of the main causes of the stressful life. It is one of the most negative emotions if not controlled with proper awareness. This page in your journal helps you to do that. The first thing you need to do is, take some deep breathe and relax. Then, make a list of things and people behind your anger. And forgive them one by one. Forgiveness expresses love and strength. As you know, "Forgiveness doesn't change the past, but it changes the future." Once done with the forgiveness practice, move to the gratefulness page. Close your eyes and find all the things and people you have in life. Write down a minimum of 10 things you are grateful for. If you are reading this book,then you are fortunate than millions of people in this world living as sightless. And if you had a meal today, then you are living a much better life than the Africans struggling for a bite of food and a sip of water. Keep counting my dear friends, you will find more and more reasons to be grateful.

Common Therapies

Stress plays the major roles in anxiety, depression, sleeping disorder and many other illnesses in life. Hectic work schedule, stressful job environment, target and deadline pressure, financial worries and relationship issues are common stress culprits. There are several ways to manage the stress and increase the ability to cope with it. Some common therapies help in stress-reduction are known as relaxation therapies.

*"A 60-minute massage is about the same as
8 hours of sleep to your body."*

A. *Massage Therapy*: Massage therapies relax your body and mind. It promotes mental relaxation and deep, peaceful sleep. These therapies boost the immunity and energy by proper rejuvenation. It improves the blood circulation and helps in detoxification. There are various types of massage that focus on a different part of the body or healing approaches. Most popular form of massages includes *Swedish massage, Aromatherapy massage, Deep tissue massage, Reflexology massage, Ayurvedic massage and Thai massage*. Swedish, Deep tissue and Aromatherapy massages are full body massages helps in muscle relax and increases blood circulation and lymph drainage. In case of Aromatherapy, the use of essential oils like lavender relaxes both the body and mind. Reflexology massages focus on the acupressure points in the foot and hands. Thai massage is a massage without oil and the therapist helps you to stretch and relax with all the different yoga poses.

B. *Salt water Therapy*: This is a simple and do-it-yourself type of therapy to clear all the negativity and get instant relaxation. After coming back from your work, take a bucket of warm water and add ½ cup of Epsom salt to the warm water. Soak your feet for 20-30 minutes twice a week to reduce stress and promote healing. Epsom salt is also known as magnesium sulphate. It has been used for hundreds of years for relaxation and healing. To get more benefits, add a fewdrops of essential oils in the water. After soaking your feet, moisturize your skin to avoid the dryness and any irritation.

C. *Cold Water Therapy*: It is also known as the cold shower therapy. It has many benefits for our body and mind. It improves blood circulation, strengthen the immune system, fight depression by reducing stress, and helps in weight loss. In ancient times, Yogis and Rishis takes cold water bath every morning to control their mind and live disease free. Now, sports people use this therapy as a recovery method for their trainings. It is also very simple to do. After your morning workout, take a cold shower for 5 minutes. You can use your bath tub by adding little ice to it for this therapy. Another advanced cold therapy method called "Cryotherapy", is a technique where the body exposed to extremely cold temperature and it has many benefits especially for athletes. They use nitrogen to decrease the temperature inside a chamber and you need to sit inside it for a few minutes. If you have the facility in your health club or gym, then try it.

D. *Ice Therapy*: It is also known as Feng Fu. It is a Chinese acupuncture technique. You need to place an ice cube on the back of your neck (Feng Fu Point) for 15 -20 minutes. Feng fu point is the point where the bottom of your skull meets your neck. It increases your overall energy, reduces stress and depression, relieves pain and improves your quality of sleep.

E. *Earthing Therapy*: Earthing is simple and easy. Just go bare foot outside and touch your feet to grass, sand, dirt or rock for at least 15-30 minutes and notice how fast stress reduces and energy improves. This connection of your feet or body to the earth's natural energy is known as Earthing or Grounding. Electrons move freely between the earth and the grounded human body. Experience this magical healing energy of the earth at work next time you are stressed or unwell.

Revise Notes

- Relaxation is nature's way of recharging. Three types of relaxation–physical, mental and complete relaxation.

- Breathing is the most simple and quick way to give relaxation to the body and mind. Various types of breathing techniques include deep breathing, diaphragm breathing, power breathing and wim-hoff breathing.

- Schedule your sleep and improve the sleep quality. Sleep and Sex both gives relaxation to the body and mind.

- Fasting is a natural healer; it relaxes the internal systems of our body. Relax your body with some body massages and therapies.

For more on relaxation, visit: *youtube.com/alokdwibedy*

Action Exercise

1. Write some effective ways to relax your body and mind.

2. Are you good with deep breathing or pranayama?

3. Mention a day of this week to do a fast? What type of fast?

4. Write your sleep schedule–start & end time?

5. Find some massage therapist in your area and book a massage.

MOTIVATION

"The only place where success comes before work is in the dictionary."

—Vidal Sassoon

"People often say that motivation doesn't last. Well, neither does bathing–that's why we recommend it daily."

—ZigZiglar

According to a study and research, 80% of New Year fitness resolution failed within the next 3-4 months. Most of the diets fail in the very first few months, and over 80% of people regain their weight. The main fundamental reasons behind these failures are lack of motivation and a strong WHY. We generally focus on all other aspects of fitness and ignore the power of daily motivation and challenges. Some of my clients gain their weight back several times a year, but with the help of daily motivation and calls, they bounce back and stay fit again and again. As you know, "Consistency is the mother of mastery", you must have a beautiful start and a strong commitment to your fitness goals. It's better to do a little exercise daily than a few hours on the weekends. Motivation works in two ways–intrinsic and extrinsic. For intrinsic motivation or self-motivation, you need to find a strong why or reason to achieve your fitness goal or to be fit and healthy. You are reading this chapter, which means you are self-motivated to read and complete this book. Great job! Keep going. For extrinsic one, you need to hire a personal coach or a fitness trainer with ample expertise in all areas of health and fitness. Another way to add consistency to your fitness and health goal is to find a partner with a similar goal or target. Most of the sports people and celebrities have their personal trainer and motivational coaches to help them achieve their goals. Let's learn some powerful ways to add motivation in your life to be healthy and fit.

Let's live to inspire...

Triangle of Success & Happiness

To achieve success in different stages of life and to get happiness is the greatest reason to be alive and staying motivated in each and every moment. To get success and happiness, what you need is a perfect balance and co-ordination of these three things, healthy body, peaceful mind, and a perfect career/craft. I call this "The Triangle of Success & Happiness".

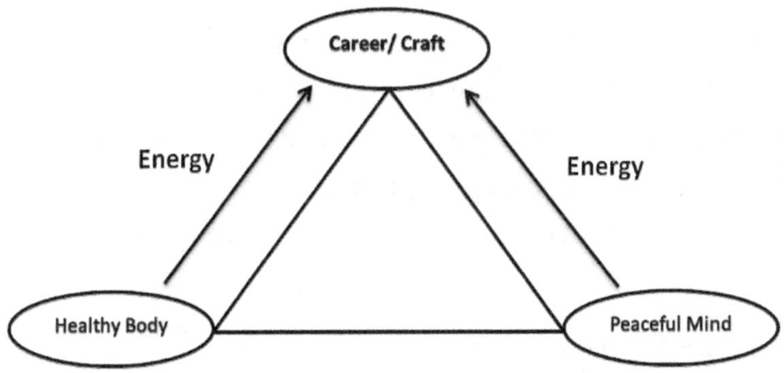

As a triangle has three points and all the points are interconnected, this triangle of success & happiness has also three points and all are interconnected. If you don't have a healthy body, then you can't concentrate in your work. And if you don't have a peaceful mind, then you will face many health issues and indecisions in your day-to-day life and career. And, if you don't enjoy your career, you will be always stressful and that will impact your body and mind. As you know, a triangle has a base with two points; this triangle has the base with a healthy body and peaceful mind. From the base, you get the energy to invest in your career/craft. Once I understood the magic of this triangle and its impact on my health, career and relationship, I got enough motivation to take care of my body and mind. Believe me, if you just follow the book and take care of your body and mind, then all other goals of your life will achievable.

Health is a Choice

I always tell my clients, "Health is a choice. Either you choose healthy or unhealthy; there is no other way". The food in your plate is health promoting or disease promoting. Whether you choose an active lifestyle or a sedentary one, choice is yours and it impacts your overall health. Let's talk on some powerful formula on choice and decision.

(A) **A + C + D = O**

Here, A–Awareness, C–Choices, D–Decision and O–Outcome/Result

Every minute of your every hour of your each day, you are facing different choices. What to eat, what not to eat. What to think, what not to think. What to do, what not to do. You are taking decisions on these small choices and these tiny decisions later convert into a great success or failure.

"It is in your moments of decision that your destiny is shaped."

—Tony Robbins

And, to take these powerful small decisions you need a great level of awareness and knowledge on the choices and its consequences. That's why, awareness is the key. To being present and having knowledge on your key areas, is important to achieve your greatness.

(B) **E + R = O**

Here, E–Event, R–Response, O–Outcome/Result

This powerful formula shows the importance of response in your life. You are going through many small events (~ Choices) in your day-to-day life. And, your outcome depend on how you respond to particular events. Like, you decide today to exercise first thing in the morning from tomorrow. After you wake up, you find the weather is too cold in the morning and you postpone it and become a victim of your procrastination. The result you know, you gain weight. Here, you don't have control over the event or result; you have only control over your response. As Lord Krishna says, "do your niskam karma without worrying about the result, you won't suffer the consequences."

"Health is a matter of choice, not a mystery of chance."

—Aristotle

(C) Delaying Gratification

This is a powerful technique to increase your willpower and raise your mindset. It means the ability to postpone your immediate pleasure to get the real happiness later. For example, you are on a fitness goal to get six packs, then you can eat the French fries now or you practice the delaying gratification and postpone it to your next cheat meal. I applied this formula to achieve many of my health and fitness goals. So, next time when some obstacles come in your process, then don't forget to practice this magical formula.

Raise your Standard

Someone well said, "Raise your standard, and the universe will meet you there." Raise your standard means elevate yourself or improve the lifestyle you are living. In this universe, each one is vibrating in their respective energy level. The simplest formula to achieve anything is enhancing your energy level to that level to feel the vibration. In this universe, it always requires that to match certain standards to achieve the greatness.

"Show me where you spend your time, money and energy and I'll tell you what you worship..."

—John Wimber

Energy is the new currency

Now, while writing this book, I am working with two start-ups as a co-founder and health coach. Starting from business to handling the customer care team to checking the products quality, it's a tough job. Writing the book on time and discussing with the publishing team is making the days longer. The only problem is the time. We have only 24 hours a day, and can't extend it. The only way to accomplish more in a limited time is by increasing the energy and productivity. If you have more energy, you can do more and achieve more with a very little prioritised rest. Energy is the outcome of these two elements–healthy body and peaceful mind. If you have energy then after a hectic work day, still you can give some time to your family, passion or any hobbies. For this, you not only have to focus on increasing the energy, you must focus on protecting it too.

There are three types of people you spend your most time with in your job and life. They are, *inspiring people, neutral people and the energy vampires.* Inspiring people are those who help you increase your current energy level through inspiration and positivity. After spending a little time with them, you feel up. Neutral people are those who are neither increase your energy nor soak your energy. Mostly, they are our family members and close friends. The energy vampires, they soak a lot of energy in a little time. They are negative people, always in stress, anxiety and complaining or blaming mood. Try to protect your energy by staying away from them. To elevate your energy level, just try to surround with these five types of people: *the inspired, the passionate, the motivated, the grateful and the open-minded.*

Raise your energy with the ages

Few months back I called my parent and asked them to come to Pune. You know what they replied, "It's so far from here (Bhubaneswar). We don't have such health conditions to go by train or even flight." That means they don't have that energy level to travel so far. After a few hours, I saw news on 3rd anniversary of Demonetisation and watched the debate. Just after that, a thought came to my mind, "Our PM Mr. Narendra Modi is 5 years older than my father." He is travelling the entire world, working 16-18 hours a day and even taking part in adventurous TV shows. Then I come up with a list that includes Amitabh Bachchan, Donald Trump, Richard Branson, Stephen King and the great Al Pacino. What's the difference then? These great masters raised their energy with the ages. When I discussed this with my clients, the most common excuses came, "They are rich. They have their own doctors, trainers and coaches. Please don't compare with them." It's not about comparing with the celebrities; it's all about their lifestyle and delaying the cheap gratification to achieve their big dreams. Even if they have their trainers and coaches, you know very well they can't hire someone to exercise or meditate for them. They have to do the practices regularly with self-discipline and perseverance.

There is a triangle called time, money and energy diagram. It explains the funny things about our life from childhood to old age through youth. When we are a child, we have lots of energy and time but missing the money. We depend upon our parents for each and everything. When we become young and started working, we get the money to spend and have energy too but have little time. We have only some weekends and few leaves for the year. And when we become old, we have time and money too but lacking the energy to enjoy the remaining part of the life. You may be in your 20s, 30s or 40s, you can raise your energy level with the ages by just following these five simple facts you just read. In the end, it's all about your choices and decisions.

Time:	✓	✗	✓
Money:	✗	✓	✓
Energy :	✓	✓	✗

1000 mile journey start with a single step

"A journey of a thousand miles begins with a single step."

—Lao Tzu

One funniest thing I observed in my clients that, they know everything and aware about the importance of health in their life. Still, they don't do the right thing and have many excuses for that. They always look for an inciting incident or some people to remind them what they already knew. Remember, it's never too late to start your fitness journey. The Ultra-athlete and fitness advocate Rich Roll started his fitness journey at 42 and became the top 25 fittest person in the world by the age of 48. To achieve that level of fitness, you don't need any super power; just you have to focus on the basics.

Little Things Matter

As you already know, every moment of your day, you face a choice. You can take a positive or negative action. And these small simple actions, repeated over time will determine the life you lead. Little things that lead to success are easy to do. Small actions compound over time give the compound or ripple effect. For example, if you exercise for an hour a day, you won't see much difference after a couple of days or even a week. But after a few months, by doing the same simple actions, you will notice a big difference. A little effort each day will bring huge rewards. Just start with 1 push up, 1 minute meditation,

1 minute walk or 1 set of exercise today and just repeat it tomorrow. It's that damn simple. No more excuses and as Nike says, "Just do it."

Knowing vs. Doing

Knowing how to do something and doing it are two different things. It's often a lot easier not to do the simple things. You need to take the right actions that lead to your destination every single day. There is a very little difference between information and knowledge. By reading a book, you are just getting the information but to gain the knowledge, you have to apply the concepts in your life and experience it. Once you experience the result, it will be much easier to differentiate between right and wrong actions. As Alcoholic Anonymous says, "Doing the same thing again and again, and expecting a different result is called Insanity", you can't repeat the same actions again that mislead you to reach your destination.

Celebrating Success

"Make time to celebrate your accomplishments,
no matter how big or small."

Life is a journey, not a destination. You need to celebrate every moment of your short and unpredictable life. The best way to celebrate in life is to set small achievable goals to grow in life. As someone said, "Don't go through life, grow through life." Like after coming back from hospital and depression, I set a goal to become an expert in the health and fitness and to help 1 million people through my services. This little book is an outcome of that goal and I will celebrate the launching day with my friends, family and you. Through this 5 year process, I sacrificed many weekends and vacations for the research and learning. Now, it's time for celebrating my success. You can set some health goals, career goals or financial goals now and have a grand celebration once achieve that, irrespective of how small the goals are.

Celebration vs. Entertainment

For success and happiness, you must know the difference between celebrations vs. entertainment. Celebration is participation. We take part and involve in happiness, while in entertainment others celebrate and we just witness the celebration. There is no involvement of our emotions in case of entertainment. Now, entertainment is so cheap and has become a part of our life like watching a movie, weekend parties, musical concerts, celebrity gossips and various stage shows. See, what you are doing here is, becoming a witness for others achievement or celebration and sharing them on social media. If you want success and happiness, then replace this cheap entertainment with the grand celebration. Just delay these instant gratifications to celebrate instead of entertain. For example, set a goal to have a certain weight or a six-pack abs, and once achieved, call your friends and family to celebrate that. Or set a goal like writing a book or building a business, once achieved the target, throw a grand celebration.

Sharing is Caring

Achievement gives success while service gives fulfilment. As Tony Robbins said, "Success without fulfilment is the ultimate failure." Nature shows us the power to serve and share. To be healthy and happy, you must learn the magic of sharing. Celebrate the success and share with others to get the fulfilment. You can share your money, your time and your skill or expertise with others. Once you complete this book, apply these concepts to enhance your health and energy and then share your learning with others. You can donate few books to your friends and family so you can make yourself healthy, your family healthy and your society and country healthy.

Revise Notes

- Three things you need to have a wonderful life– healthy body, peaceful mind and fulfilled career.
- Remember, health is a choice and lifestyle is the new medicine.

$$E + R = O; A + C + D = O$$

- Energy is the new currency. Increase the energy with the ages and raise your standard.
- Know the difference between information and knowledge. An ounce of practice is much better that loads of theory.

To know more on Motivation, visit:
youtube.com/alokdwibedy

Action Exercises

1. Draw the triangle of success & happiness in a sheet and paste it in your room.

2. What are the decisions you will take to improve your health?

3. How's your current energy level? What actions will you take to raise your standard?

4. Make a promise note that you will take care of your health from today onwards.

5. Decide a day when you are planning to start the 5 week fitness challenge. Is it today?

Summary

We had started our fitness journey with my story and few promises to make ourselves healthy, our family healthy and our society or country healthy. In the last few days, we learned the five basic facts to be healthy and fit. Now, I assume you already got a few concepts and applied to see some results out of it. Let's revise the concepts once last time.

1–First fact is Exercise

Exercise is a miracle drug because of its many benefits for our body and mind. Do a quick workout in the morning to improve the circulation and elevate the energy level. Track your steps to reach the magic number–10,000 steps each day. Our body releases toxins through sweating so, sweat more while exercising. Don't forget to do a 2X workout after your job to release all the stress. Find the best exercise for you and just do it daily.

2–Second fact is Nutrition

As you know, food is the medicine, focus on your regular meals. Always choose nutrient-dense, high pranic foods like fruits, vegetables, nuts, seeds, greens and sprouts. Don't go for any temporary fad-diet; just do the best lifestyle changes. Detox your body regularly and add super foods and greens in your diet.

3–Third fact is Meditation

Exercise is for body, meditation is for mind. Understand your mind and make a manual for this wonderful machine. Try different meditations and make your own model for practice. Remember, Mindfulness is a 24*7 meditation.

4–Fourth fact is Relaxation

When the body and mind are constantly overworked, their natural efficiency diminishes. Relaxation is also an important pillar of our lifestyle as exercise and nutrition. Do some breathing exercise and focus on your sleep quality to relax more. Fasting is a best way for physical and mental relaxation. Go for a weekly body massage or any therapies to give your body some relaxation.

5–Fifth fact is Motivation

Focus on both intrinsic and extrinsic motivation. Find your why or purpose to have a constant self-motivation. For extrinsic motivation, find a personal trainer or coach who can guide and inspire you. Remember both the formulae, A+C+D = O & E+R = O. Raise your standard by increasing your energy level.

Once learned and understood these facts, the two things you need in your life are self-discipline and consistency. You need to discipline with the schedule and lifestyle. You are responsible for your life. Success and failure don't depend on your luck but your choices, your small daily choices. With each decision, either you are moving towards success or failures. And in this roller-coaster journey, you definitely face some challenges. Don't think to quit. In that moment, just recall why you started the journey. Be consistent with your daily practices. And within a few years, you will become unstoppable. Practice these five facts and add to your lifestyle to live a legendary life with full of health, happiness and fulfilment.

5 Week Fitness Challenge

Thank you again for reading this book and completing it. Let's take the last step to convert the information into knowledge. This is a challenge to you for the next 5 weeks. I will become your personal coach and give you few tasks to complete to take your fitness to the next level. Game on!! You can also check our team in the let's connect page for the one-on-one coaching program with me. Believe me, it will not only change your health but also can change your life. See you!!

Week 1

Exercise – Go for a 20-30 minute walk in the morning. You can do brisk walk, power walk or even incline walk or hiking.

Nutrition– Start your day with the detox drink. Green juices are best for detox like wheatgrass, amla, carrot, beetroot, tulsi, neem, or any seasonal fruit juices. But the best one to have is wheatgrass juice on empty stomach.

Meditation – Start practicing breathe meditation for at least 5-10 minutes. Sit comfortably in a quiet place and observe your breathes.

Relaxation – Do water therapy after your work. Take a bucket of warm water, add ½ cup Epsom salt and soak your feet for 20 minutes with your favourite music or any meditation music.

Motivation – Find an accountability partner for your health and fitness. Share your goal with them and promise that you are going to follow these 5 week challenge.

Week 2

Exercise – Add some rounds of Surya-Namaskar to your walking. You can do before or after coming back from walking. Or you can just do few rounds of Surya-Namaskar with some basic yoga poses.

Nutrition – Add lots of colourful and seasonal Fruits in your breakfast and mid-morning snacks. You can add fruits like apple, orange, banana, pear, papaya, pineapple, pomegranate, kiwi, guava or any seasonal fruits in your breakfast bowl, salad, smoothies or juices.

Meditation – Practice walking meditation this week. While walking, observe the point when your feet touched the ground. Feel it and even synchronise your breathing with the steps. Check the meditation chapter to know more.

Relaxation – Go for cold-water bath after your morning walk or exercise. Take cold-shower for 5 minutes daily.

Motivation – Watch any 1 -2 documentaries on health and fitness.

Week 3

Exercise – Add anti-gravity exercises to your routine this week. Start with few jumping exercises like inclined walking, hiking or stair climbing.

Nutrition –Eat a Salad in every major meals of your day. Start the meal by eating the salad first. In breakfast you can have fruit salad and in the lunch and dinner, add a raw vegetable salad. Cucumber, Carrot, Tomato, Beet, Cabbage, Onion and Lettuce are best to add in vegetable salad.

Meditation – Let's start mantra meditation or chanting this week. Decide your favourite mantra or get the mantra initiation from a Guru. Chant the mantra mentally for few minutes daily with full faith and believe. You can choose mantras like, "Om Namah Sivaya", "Om Namoh Narayanaya".

Relaxation – Practice complete relaxation like savasana or auto-suggestion few minutes daily in the morning or evening every day in this week. Best time to practice this relaxation technique is just after your workout or before sleep.

Motivation – Read 1 life-changing self-help book in this week. The book I am reading while writing this line is, "Tuesday with Morie".

Week 4

Exercise – Add few strength and flexibility exercises this week. No, you don't require a gym membership for this, use your body-weight and start from your home. Body weight exercises like pushups, squats, planks and burpees are best to start with. For flexibility, start with few basic yoga asanas. If possible, hire a personal trainer for first few weeks.

Nutrition – Take care of your snacks. We often add many unhealthy stuffs and extra calories in both mid-morning and evening snacks. In mid-morning snacks, have a piece of fruit or few pieces of fruits with your favourite nut butter. In evening snacks, have a handful of nuts and seeds with your favourite herbal tea. Or you can go for a sprout salad as well.

Meditation –As you know, concentration always comes before meditation. Let's practice few concentration exercises this week. Start with the Trataka exercise. It is a yogic method of concentration that involves staring at a single focus point like a black dot or candle flame. Also, you can improve your concentration by observing the petals of a flower or second hand of your watch.

Relaxation – Go for an early morning hike or spend few hours in the nature in this week. Remember, Nature heals us in many ways. Surrender your body, mind and soul to the nature at least once or twice this week and see the difference!

Motivation – You are average of five people you are associated with. So, mind your association in this week and spend most of your quality time with fit and uplifting people.

Week 5

Exercise – Call your buddy and find a group. Start playing your favourite childhood games now at least once or twice a week. You can play in the morning or in the weekends. Believe me, this is the best exercise for your body and mind. Yes, here, I am talking about outdoor games like cricket, football, badminton, tennis, basketball, and volley ball.

Nutrition – Here, let's delete few things from your diet and kitchen. Delete all the highly-processed or refined food items like refined sugar, refined oil, sugary drinks, or any packaged foods like biscuits, cakes or chips.

Meditation – Mindfulness is the master of all meditation. It's like practicing meditation 24*7. Add few meditation techniques to your day-to-day activities. For example, while brushing your teeth, just remind yourself that throughout the day, you are going to speak softly and chew your foods properly.

Relaxation – Find a nearest spa in your town. Book a full body massage for this week. You can choose Swedish massage or Aromatherapy massage with lavender oil to be pain-free and relax.

Motivation – Remember, Consistency is the key and Fitness is a journey. To be fit and healthy, you need to follow these facts throughout your lifetime. Keep this book with you and re-read once or twice a month for a constant reminder. All the very best and would love to see you on the top!!

AD's Lifestyle Program

As you know, "Dieting is temporary and Lifestyle is permanent". This is a special lifestyle program that helps you to lose weight, get more energy, and avoid many lifestyle diseases. If you follow this lifestyle plan, then you can protect yourself from diabetes, heart diseases, blood pressure, cancer, and depression. If you are suffering from these diseases, then through this lifestyle you can reverse the diseases. The most important thing about this lifestyle plan is, it's very simple to follow and you can do it for lifetime.

This program is a weekly program divided into three sections. Once done for one week, just repeat the same for a lifetime.

Section 1 [Monday - Friday or 5 days a week]

For these 5 days, you just need to follow a normal lifestyle with your favourite foods. Follow the plan as per the instruction.

Detox Drink–Oil-pull for 10-15 minutes and then brush your teeth. Start your day with a detox drink. Simple lemon water is also okay. For best results, go for vegetable juices in the morning.

Plan Your Day–As you know, "Failing to plan is planning to fail." Before marching towards your day, plan the activities. It will improve your productivity and help you achieve your goals on time. You can plan while having your detox drink.

Empty stomach Workout–After the detox drink and planning, it's time to give your body the best gift–a quick workout for strength, cardiac health and flexibility. As Spartan warrior said, "Sweat more in training, Bleed less in Battle". Do the workout in the park or outside to soak the morning sun.

Cold water Bath–Give your body a challenge. Your body loves it. Instead of usual bath, go for a cold-water bath and feel the meditative state. It works a best recovery method for your quick workout and activates the brown fat.

Breakfast [8–10 am]–Till the time, your body cries for nutrients. Fill it with a healthy-balanced breakfast. It must include complex carb, protein, healthy fat and the micros. Best options are Oatmeal bowl, a fruit & nut Smoothie, Green Juices or any regional healthy breakfast options.

Mid-morning snacks–If feeling hungry at your work then only have a piece of fruits else skip it. Fruits in the mid-morning snacks provide the much-needed fibre before lunch. Go for a quick walk for 10-15 minute in the sun to get the melatonin and vitamin-D.

Lunch [1- 2pm]–Start your lunch with a few deep breaths. It activates the parasympathetic nervous systems to improve the digestion. Have your green salad first for the prebiotic and then have the balanced lunch with rice/roti, dal, veggies, curd or chutney. Have some fennel seeds without sugar or 1-2 cloves after your lunch.

Power Breathing–It's not how you start but how you finish matters. To finish well, you need little pump-up towards the evening. Power breathing is a great way to increase your energy and focus. Go for a quick walk and do some deep breathing in the afternoon.

Evening Snacks–In evening snacks have a cup of herbal tea or black coffee with a handful of nuts and seeds. It gives a good support to your low-calorie dinner and a pre-workout for your 2X workout. You can have a bowl of sprout salad.

2X Workout–Release all the stresses and anxieties by a quick walk or an exercise session after your job. It releases all the happy hormones to give much-needed relaxation to wind-up the day. Don't do vigorous exercises close to your bed time.

Dinner [6–8 pm]–Have a very light dinner. An overloaded gut before sleep leads to fight with the brain. A well-balanced salad with lentils and veggies is a good option. Else, you can go for a small meal. And by doing dinner a little early, you are doing Intermittent fasting daily and giving the rest and maintenance to your digestive system.

Read Book–To have a quality sleep, you need to switch off all the electronic devices at least 1 -2 hour of your bed time. The best things to do before sleep is to read a paperback book especially self-help or biographies. Do a quick meditation to control your thought waves. And By this, you own the day. Congratulation!!

Section 2 [Saturday or 1 Day a week]

Fasting Day–After 5 days of eating, it's time to give rest to your gut and digestive system. You can water fast, juice fast or even dry fast depending upon your goal and capacity. Remember, 1 day of dry fast is equal to 3 day of water fast.

Internet Fasting–Once in a week, you must switch off your Wi-Fi and go for a screen Sabbath. You can use some times in your most creative work in this day. Just stay away from all social media feeds and spend some quality family and friends time today.

Detox Massage–"Leaders and Winners don't have off days, they have relaxed days." They take a day off to relax and rejuvenate for the upcoming work week. Book your weekly message or any therapies and have 1-2 hours of relaxation today.

Media Detox–Not only social media but avoid any other media like a newspaper, magazines or TV in this day of the week. It's required for mental relaxation.

Practice Yoga& Meditation–To get maximum benefit of this relax day, do a little of yoga and meditation in the morning or evening. If possible, hire a trainer or join a class for this.

Section 3 [Sunday or 1 day a week]

Raw Food Day–You already detox your body yesterday with a fasting, massage and yoga practices. Your body need purest form of food today to nourish your cells. Go for a complete raw food diet today. You can have green juices, smoothies, salads, nuts and seeds, soups and herbal teas.

Plan Your Week–Usually, we consider Sunday is the first day of the week. Spend some "me-time" to plan your week. You can do it any day once per week to track your progress.

The Mission

After getting the formulae for the health and energy, I started working with a mission. For this mission, I had to quit my daily job. And the mission is, "To make yourself healthy, your family healthy, and your society and country healthy". As a writer, speaker and trainer, the aim is to uplift 1 million people's life through my writing, speaking and coaching. Another element of the mission is to make health and fitness simple by clearing all the confusions.

In addition to this, our mission is to spend a percentage of profits from each copy of this book to non-profit charities, cancer patients and hospitals and with the needy people in hospitals and education systems.

Thank You So Much for being part of our journey and mission and your valuable support.

Let's Connect

Alok Dwibedy (AD) is a fitness nutritionist, health and lifestyle coach, Yoga trainer and Juice therapist. After quitting his job in an MNC, he dedicated his life for inspiring people to live a life with health, happiness and fulfilment. He is a writer, speaker and coach.

Loves to read, write, speak and watch documentaries.

If you enjoyed the book and would like to connect AD, you can reach him at,

YouTube: *youtube/alokdwibedy*

Facebook: *Alok Dwibedy*

Instagram: *Alok Dwibedy_ad*

Email: *fivefactfitness@gmail.com*

Website: *www.alokdwibedy.com*

Book AD to Speak

Book AD to speak at your event in school, colleges, corporates or clubs and he's guaranteed to deliver inspiring and life-changing experience for everyone with his beautiful true story and full of energy!

Few talks of AD

- Five Facts of Fitness

- Triangle of Success & Happiness

- Discover Yourself

- Machine without Manual – MIND

- Ditch your "Busy-ness" & improve Productivity

To bring these talks to your organisation – please write to *alokdwibedy@focus.com/fivefactfitness@gmail.com.*